Yes, You Can Speak Korean!

BOOK
2

Yes, You Can Speak Korean!

Daniel Y. Jang & Jacob S. Jang

Hollym

Elizabeth, NJ·Seoul

Yes, You Can Speak Korean! (Book 2)

First published in 2008
by Hollym International Corp.
18 Donald Place, Elizabeth, NJ 07208, U.S.A.
Phone: (908) 353-1655   Fax: (908) 353-0255
http://www.hollym.com

한림출판사
Hollym

Published simultaneously in Korea
by Hollym Corporation; Publishers
13-13 Gwancheol-dong, Jongno-gu, Seoul 110-111, Korea
Phone: (02) 735-7551~4   Fax: (02) 730-5149, 8192
http://www.hollym.co.kr   e-Mail: info@hollym.co.kr

ISBN: 978-1-56591-236-6
Library of Congress Control Number: 2006929307

Printed in Korea

PREFACE

This book was written based on the co-author's experiences teaching Korean to his children who were born and raised in America.

I wrote this book with my son after he graduated from college because we wanted to share our lessons learned with others so that they, too, could learn Korean more easily.

Every parent's desire is to raise and educate his or her child in the best ways possible, but in reality this task is not an easy one. What should parents teach their children, and at what point should they begin the process? What are the best methods for teaching children? These are just some of the questions with which parents struggle, especially as it relates to teaching children languages.

Despite not being an expert in linguistics education, I took proactive steps to encourage my son to learn how to speak and read Korean early on, instead of simply letting him learn naturally as he got older. When my son began to say his first words, I made flashcards so that he would become familiar with various words, their sounds, and their associated pictures. As we reviewed more and more flashcards, he improved in cognition, his vocabulary increased, and by the age of two he was reading simple Korean books.

As our family spent meaningful time playing word games with our son using the flashcards each evening, my son naturally gained more familiarity with books and reading in this environment. By the age of three, he also learned many English words and began reading simple books in English as well. Shortly thereafter, he won a prize for his recital of a story called "The Duck and the Fox" in a Korean storytelling contest held in New York. That same year, he delivered a speech entitled "Why Should We Learn Korean?" at the annual Washington D.C. Korean Language School convention. When my son turned four, I attempted to teach him Chinese characters also using these flashcards, and after three months, he was able to read 200 characters as well. These flashcards were proving to be a successful and effective method of teaching my son how to read.

I am sharing these stories with you now so that you too can make use of these methods and this book to give your son or daughter confidence in their learning experience. This book has been developed based on the same methods as using those flashcards with my son. Specifically, it teaches students how to read Korean using the Phonics system in the same way many children learn how to read English. It is the easiest way to teach children who already speak and read English to learn Korean. In addition, the lessons are organized in a systematic fashion, so that children in Korea can begin learning Korean using these books (This book is not necessarily designed for use by children on their own).

This is the best book for those first learning how to read Korean with correct pronunciation, including for Korean Americans, exchange students, foreigners, and many others.

Daniel Y. Jang & Jacob S. Jang

How to Use Book 2

Yes, You Can Speak Korean! is a two-volume textbook series designed primarily to teach students how to read Korean. As students learn how to read proficiently, they will also learn basic vocabulary, grammar and expressions. This series, unlike others, is written in a style specifically designed to be familiar for students growing up in the United States. Students will be more accustomed to the American Phonics method, explanations, and exercises used in this series. *Yes, You Can Speak Korean!* can be used at home, with the help of parents, or at a Korean Language School.

For ages 6+: Each lesson contains a new reading passage, suggested classwork and homework. Students should focus primarily on being able to read each lesson's passage fluidly, with ease. Parents/Teachers may choose to emphasize vocabulary, grammar, and/or expressions, as desired and appropriate. To avoid confusion, passages only contain key grammatical concepts that have been introduced in previous lessons.

Contents

Let's Continue to Study
Korean in Book 2!

Let's Learn about the Family!

Come and meet my family. I've got a dad, mom and an older sister, named Dorothy. But there are six people who live in my house. Can you guess the other two?

I. 가족 (Family)

할아버지와 할머니,
아버지와 어머니, 누나와 나,
우리 가족은 모두 여섯입니다.

New Vocabulary

할아버지 grandfather	···와 ··· and
할머니 grandmother	아버지(아빠) father (dad)
어머니(엄마) mother (mom)	누나 older sister
나 I, me	우리 we, our
가족 family	모두 all together
여섯 six	···입니다(이다) to be (am, are, is)

Grammar and Notes

Vocabulary

Names of Family Members

Dad's side	삼촌 uncle	고모 aunt	사촌 cousin
Mom's side	외삼촌 uncle	이모 aunt	외사촌 cousin
For boys	형 older bro.	누나 older sis.	동생 younger
For girls	오빠 older bro.	언니 older sis.	형제,자매 sibling

Grammar

The Usage of 와, 과 (*and*)

와 and 과 both mean <u>and</u>, but they are used in different cases.

Case 1: After a final consonant, use 과.
- for example, after 집

eg. 집과 아파트
팔과 다리

Case 2: After a vowel (no final consonant), use 와.
- for example, after 지

eg. 할아버지와 할머니
아버지와 어머니

Translation

There are all together six people in my family: grandfather and grandmother, father and mother, and my sister and me.

Classwork and Homework

1. Fill in the boxes with the correct conjunction. Use 와 or 과.

할아버지 ☐ 할머니

코리 ☐ 도로시

어머니 ☐ 아버지

한국 ☐ 미국

손 ☐ 발

2. Match the word on the left with its meaning on the right.

가족 ○   ○ sister

누나 ○   ○ all

모두 ○   ○ family

할아버지 ○   ○ grandfather

3. On a separate sheet of paper, draw your family tree.

Let's Learn How to Greet!

Did you meet my family? Great. Well, aren't you going to say hi? Don't be shy. Come say hi!

2. 인사 (Greeting)

"안녕하세요?"

"안녕."

좋은 아침입니다.

우리는 서로 인사합니다.

New Vocabulary

안녕/안녕하세요 hello	좋은(좋다) good
아침 morning	서로 each other
인사합니다(인사하다) to greet	

Grammar and Notes

Vocabulary Most Frequently Used Greetings

안녕 - Hi / Bye (informal)

안녕하세요? / 안녕하십니까?

Hello (formal).
Use when you meet people.

안녕히 가세요. / 안녕히 가십시오.

lit. I hope you'll have a pleasant journey; Goodbye (formal).
Use when the other person is leaving.

안녕히 계세요. / 안녕히 계십시오.

lit. I hope you'll have a pleasant stay; Goodbye (formal).
Use when you are leaving and the other person is staying.

Translation

"Hello?" / "Hi."
It is a good morning.
We greet each other.

Classwork and Homework

❖ **Directions:** When people get together, they first exchange greetings to each other. Suppose you are a student and the other person is an adult. Match the correct greeting for each situation.

1. When you meet an adult,

   You say to the adult, ○   ○ "안녕."

   The adult says to you, ○   ○ "안녕하세요."

2. When you leave,

   You say to the adult, ○   ○ "안녕히 계세요."

   The adult says to you, ○   ○ "잘 가."

3. When the other person leaves,

   You say to the adult, ○   ○ "잘 있어."

   The adult says to you, ○   ○ "안녕히 가세요."

Let's Take a Look around the House!

Did you say hi to my family? Then, what are you waiting for? Come on in. Let me show you around my house!

3. 집 (House)

새집으로 이사합니다.

새집에는 방, 부엌, 식당이 있습니다.

새집에는 창고도 있습니다.

New Vocabulary

새집 new house	…으로 to, towards
이사합니다(이사하다) to move	방 room, bedroom
부엌 kitchen	식당 dining room
있습니다(있다) there is/are	창고 garage; storage room
…도 also/too	

Grammar and Notes

Phrase

있다 / 있습니다 / 있어요(*There is / are*)

Ex. 집이 **있습니다**(**있어요**). *There is a house.*

Vocabulary

Things around the House

화장실 bathroom   지하실 basement
계단 stairs   정원 garden

Grammar

···에, ···에는, ···에서 indicate place or location.

1) ···에(는) can mean "at" or "in."

새집에 방이 있어요. *There is a room in the new house.*
새집에는 방이 있어요. *In the new house there is a room.*
어머니는 집에 있어요. *Mom is at home.*

2) ···에 can mean "to."

나는 학교에 가요. *I go to school.*

3) ···에서 can mean "from."

오빠가 학교에서 와요. *My brother comes from school.*

Translation

We are moving to a new house. In the new house, there is a room, a kitchen, and a dining room. In the new house, there is also a garage.

22

1. Reading Comprehension: Answer these questions about the story.

   1) What are there in Kory's new house?

   2) Is there a garage too?

2. Fill in the blanks with the given word, using the phrase that means "there is/are."

   1) 집 [　] [이] [있] [　] [　] .

   2) 식당 [　] [　] [이] [　] [　] [　] [　] .

   3) 창고 [　] [　] [가] [　] [　] [　] [　] .

3. Match each sentence with its meaning.

   1) 새집에는 부엌이 있어요. ○   ○ We move to a new house.

   2) 텔레비전이 방에 있어요. ○   ○ Grandmom is in the dining room.

   3) 우리는 새집으로 이사합니다. ○   ○ There's a kitchen in the new house.

   4) 할머니는 식당에 있어요. ○   ○ There is a television in the room.

Let's See What Things Are in My House!

I like running around inside the house. I'll race you from the living room to my bedroom. But be careful! There are a lot of things in the room. Don't break anything!

4. 가구 (Furniture)

거실에는 소파, 테이블, 등이 있어요.
벽에는 그림과 시계가 있어요.
방에는 침대, 옷장, 거울이 있어요.

Good thing you didn't break any of those things. Whew, I'm tired from the race. Let's play again tomorrow. I'll see you in the morning!

New Vocabulary

소파 sofa	테이블 table	등 lamp
거실 living room	그림 picture	시계 clock
벽 wall	침대 bed	옷장 closet
거울 mirror		

Grammar and Notes

···있다 / 있습니다 / 있어요 (*There is / are*)

···없다 / 없습니다 / 없어요 (*There is / are no*)

1) 방에는 소파가 **있어요**. *There is a sofa in the bedroom.*
   방에는 소파가 **없어요**. *There is no sofa in the bedroom.*

2) 거실에는 침대가 **있어요**. *There is a bed in the living room.*
   거실에는 침대가 **없어요**. *There is no bed in the living room.*

Vocabulary

Prepositions for Location

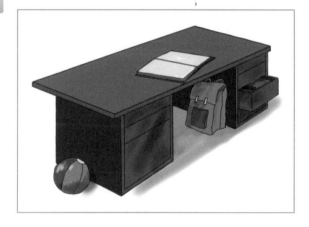

앞에(in front of)
뒤에(behind)
안에(inside)
위에(on top of)
밑에(under)
옆에(next to)

Ex. 책상 **위에** 책이 있습니다.   *There is a book on top of the desk.*
    책상 **밑에** 가방이 있습니다.   *There is a bag under the desk.*

Translation

In the living room, there is a sofa, a table, and a lamp. On the wall, there is a picture and a clock. In the bedroom, there is a bed, a closet, and a mirror.

Classwork and Homework

1. Using the words in the box below, fill in the blanks.

방에, 벽에, 부엌에

1) 어머니는 ☐☐☐ 가요. *Mom goes to the kitchen.*

2) 그림이 ☐☐ 있어요. *The picture is on the wall.*

3) 나는 ☐☐ 있어요. *I am in the room.*

2. Change the sentences to the negative form.

Ex. 시계가 있어요. *There is a watch.*

→ 시계가 없어요. *There is no watch.*

1) 그림이 있어요.
There is a picture.
☐☐☐ ☐☐☐ .

2) 소파가 있어요.
There is a sofa.
☐☐☐ ☐☐ .

3) 누나는 방에 있어요. *My sister is in the room.*

☐☐☐ ☐☐☐ ☐☐☐ .

Let's Learn Names of Parts of the Body!

Yawn! Good morning. Let me just stretch one last time. I need to stretch each part of my body, from my head to my toes. Can you reach your toes? Ahh, that feels great!

5. 몸 (Body)

얼굴에는 눈, 코, 입, 귀가 있습니다.
몸에는 팔과 다리가 있습니다.
손과 발도 있습니다.

New Vocabulary

얼굴 face	눈 eye(s)	코 nose
입 mouth	귀 ear(s)	몸 body
팔 arm(s)	다리 leg(s)	손 hand(s)
발 foot(feet)		

Grammar and Notes

Vocabulary Parts of the Body

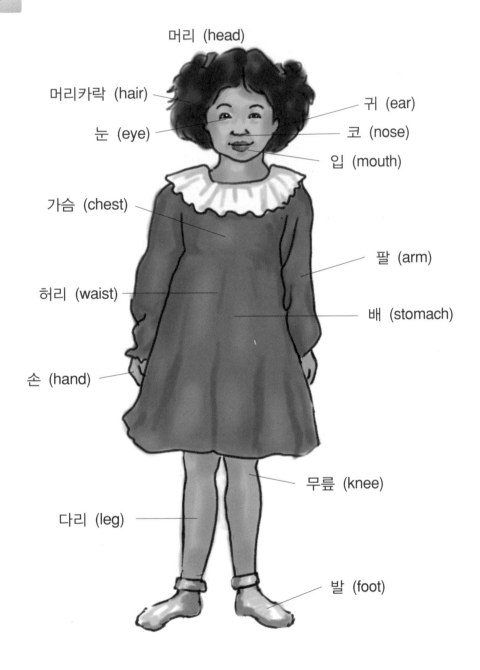

머리 (head)

머리카락 (hair)

귀 (ear)

눈 (eye)

코 (nose)

입 (mouth)

가슴 (chest)

팔 (arm)

허리 (waist)

배 (stomach)

손 (hand)

무릎 (knee)

다리 (leg)

발 (foot)

Translation On the face, there are eyes, a nose, a mouth, and ears. On the body, there are arms and legs. There are also hands and feet.

Classwork and Homework

1. Answer the following riddles.

   1) What is under your nose?

   2) What is on the side of your head?

   3) What is at the bottom of your body?

2. Match the phrases to form a complete sentence.

     몸에는 ○   ○ 눈이 있어요.

    얼굴에는 ○   ○ 발이 있어요.

    다리에는 ○   ○ 다리가 있어요.

3. Fill in the boxes with a correct conjunction. Use 와 or 과.

   눈 ☐ 코   그림 ☐ 시계

   다리 ☐ 팔   소파 ☐ 램프

   입 ☐ 귀   침대 ☐ 옷장

Let's Get Ready to Go to School!

Well, I should stop lying around in bed. I have to go to school today. Time to wash up and get ready for the day. Off to the bathroom!

6. 아침 세수 (Morning Wash)

나는 세수를 합니다.
누나가 이를 닦습니다.
우리는 머리를 빗습니다.
우리는 옷을 입습니다.

Hee, hee! It's fun to splash my sister with water. I better run away before she catches me!

New Vocabulary

나는 I	세수 washing one's face
이 tooth(teeth)	닦습니다(닦다) to brush
머리 hair	빗습니다(빗다) to comb
옷 clothes	입습니다(입다) to wear

Grammar and Notes

Grammar

Subject and Object Particles

In Korean, subjects and objects have their own particles. You can easily tell if a word is a subject or an object.

Note: Use ···은 and ···는 when you want to emphasize the subject.

1) The subject particles are ···은 / ···는 and ···이 / ···가.

  a. When the subject has a final consonant, use ···은 or ···이.
    Ex. 컵은 없어요. *There is no cup.*
    거울이 있어요. *There is a mirror.*

  b. When there is no final consonant, use ···는 or ···가.
    Ex. 누나가 와요. *My sister is coming.*
    우리는 인사합니다. *We greet each other.*

2) The object particles are ···을 / ···를.

  a. When the object has a final consonant, use ···을.
    Ex. 누나가 이를 닦습니다. *My sister brushes her teeth.*

  b. When there is no final consonant, use ···를.
    Ex. 어머니는 머리를 빗습니다. *Mom brushes her hair.*

Translation

I wash my face. My sister brushes her teeth. We comb our hair. We wear our clothes.

Classwork and Homework

1. Put the correct subject particle (···은, ···는, ···이, ···가)
   or object particle (···을, ···를) in the boxes.

   1) 아버지 ☐ 세수 ☐ 합니다.

   2) 동생 ☐ 옷 ☐ 입습니다.

   3) 나 ☐ 공부 ☐ 합니다.

   4) 옷장 ☐ 방에 있습니다.

   5) 누나 ☐ 옵니다.

2. Match the words together to form the sentence on the
   right.

   할머니가 ◦   ◦ 서로   ◦ 입어요.   ◦ My sister wears the clothes.

   누나가 ◦   ◦ 머리를   ◦ 인사합니다.   ◦ We greet each other.

   우리는 ◦   ◦ 옷을   ◦ 빗습니다.   ◦ Grandma combs her hair.

Let's Go to School!

It's time to go to school. I kind of like going to school because you get to play with friends. Sometimes, you can learn cool things, too. But I like playing better. I better hurry up before I miss the school bus! Come on. Let's go!

7. 학교 (School)

나는 학교에 갑니다.
친구들과 함께 학교에 갑니다.
우리는 학교에서 공부를 합니다.
친구들과 사이 좋게 놉니다.

New Vocabulary

학교 school	···에 to, at
갑니다(가다) to go	친구(들) friend(s)
함께 together	···에서 at
공부 study	사이 좋게 friendly
놉니다(놀다) to play	

Grammar and Notes

Grammar

Basic Sentence Structure

1) Subject + Verb (Simple Sentence)

Subject & Particle	Verb

우리는 공부합니다. *We study.*
우리는 인사합니다. *We greet.*

2) Subject + Object + Verb

Subject & Particle	Object & Particle	Verb

오빠가 이를 닦습니다. *My brother brushes his teeth.*
우리는 머리를 빗습니다. *We brush our hair.*

3) Subject + Complement + Linking Verb (···이다, ···입니다, ···에요)

Subject & Particle	Complement	Linking Verb

나는 오빠입니다. *I am an older brother.*
아빠는 선생님입니다. *Dad is a teacher.*

Do you see the differences between Korean and English?

In Korean, the verb comes very last in the sentence. Also, the verb form does not change because of number (singular or plural) or person (I, you, he/she/it).

Ex. 나는 **간다**. (Singular, 1st person) *I go.*
사람들이 **간다**. (Plural, 3rd person) *They go.*
여자가 **간다**. (Singular, 3rd person) *She goes.*

Translation

I go to school. I go to school, together with friends. We study at school. I get along well with friends.

Classwork and Homework

1. Reading Comprehension: Answer these questions about the story.

   1) Where did they go?

   2) What did they do in school?

   3) With whom did they play?

2. Rearrange the words below to make a sentence.

   1) 학교에 가요 우리는

   2) 나는 공부해요 방에서

   3) 옷을 누나는 입어요

3. Let's learn more words about school. Copy the words below.

teacher
선	생	님

desk
책	상

classroom
교	실

homework
숙	제

test/exam
시	험

English
영	어

Let's Learn Korean, a Secret Code!

What kinds of things do you learn in school? I have classes like math and reading. Oh, and I almost forgot... I have Korean class, too.

8. 한국어 시간 (Korean Class)

"이것은 무엇입니까?"
"책입니다."
"저것은 무엇입니까?"
"창문입니다."
 한국어 시간은 재미있습니다.

I think it's cool to learn another language. It's like a secret code you can use when you don't want to speak English!

New Vocabulary

이것 this	무엇 what
책 book	저것 that
창문 window	한국어 시간 Korean class
재미있습니다(재미있다) to be interesting, to be fun	

Grammar and Notes

Note: The demonstrative pronoun can not refer to a person. For a person, always use the pronoun in this way: This is my dad. 이 분은 (not 이것은) 우리 아빠입니다.

1. Demonstrative Pronouns

이것 (*this*), 그것 (*that*), 저것 (*that*)

Demonstrative pronouns refer to things.

1) They can be used with subject or object particles.
   Ex. **이것**은 책상입니다. *This is a book.*
   그것은 책입니다. *That is a book.*
   나는 **저것**을 싫어해요. *I dislike that (over there).*

2) They can be used as an adjective. Use 이, 그, 저.
   Ex. **이** 책은 커요. *This book is big.*
   그 책은 책상 위에 있어요. *That book is on the desk.*
   저 사람은 학생입니다. *That person (over there) is a student.*

2. Interrogative Sentence

Interrogative Pronouns:
누구 who
무엇 what
어디 where
언제 when
왜 why
어떻게 how

To form a question, use an interrogative pronoun and change the ending of the sentence to 까. (See also the page 50).

Ex. Q: **어디**에 갑니까? *Where do you go?*
   A: 학교에 갑니다. *I go to school.*

   Q: 저것은 **무엇**입니까? *What is that?*
   A: 그것은 책입니다. *That is a book.*

Translation

"What is this?" / "It is a book."
"What is that?" / "That is a window."
Korean class is fun.

Classwork and Homework

1. Fill in the blanks to form the sentence on the left.

   1) I like this.

   | | | | | | 좋 | 아 | 해 | 요 | .

   2) My sister likes that clothes (over there).

   | | | | | 옷 | 을 | | | | | .

   3) This is a book.

   | | 은 | | | | | .

   4) It is a picture.

   | | | | | 입 | | .

2. Fill in the blanks using 이 and 저.

   1) This room | | 방

   2) That house | | 집

   3) This nose | | 코

   4) That window | | 창 | 문

   5) This teacher | | 선 | 생 | 님

   6) That school | | 학 | 교

3. Match the questions with the correct answer.

   저분은 <u>누구</u>입니까? *Who is he?* ○   ○ 책입니다.

   <u>어디</u>에 갑니까? *Where do you go?* ○   ○ 오늘 갑니다.

   저것은 <u>무엇</u>입니까? *What is that?* ○   ○ 우리 아빠입니다.

   <u>언제</u> 갑니까? *Whcn do you go?* ○   ○ 학교에 갑니다.

Ugh! My mom told me to go run an errand. I have to go to my neighbor's house and drop something off. Come with me!

9. 심부름 (Errand)

"아주머니 계세요?"

아주머니가 안에서 나오십니다.

"어머니가 이것을 보내셨어요."

"그래, 고맙다."

"안녕히 계세요."

"그래, 잘 가."

New Vocabulary

아주머니 older lady, ma'am	계세요? Are (you) here?
안에서 from inside	나오십니다(나오다) to come out
보내셨어요(보내다) to send	그래 yes, Okay
고맙다 Thank you	잘 가 goodbye

Grammar and Notes

Vocabulary

More Greetings

Practice these expressions in a dialogue with your partner.

1) When you visit someone's house:
   계십니까?   *Is anyone here?*

2) When someone visits your house:
   어서 오세요(오십시오 / 와).   *Welcome.*

3) When you meet someone you know:
   안녕하십니까? 잘 있었니?
   Hello. How are you doing?

4) When you see someone after a long time:
   반갑습니다.   *It's good to see you.*
   오랜만입니다.   *It's been a while.*

5) When you say goodbye to the person:
   안녕히 계십시오. 잘 있어. (staying)
   안녕히 가십시오. 잘 가세요. (leaving)

6) Around meal time:
   식사하셨습니까? 진지 드셨습니까?
   Have you had (breakfast, lunch, dinner) yet?

7) In the morning after you wake up:
   안녕히 주무셨습니까? 잘 잤니?
   Good morning. (lit. Did you sleep well?)

Translation

"Ma'am, are you there?" A lady comes out from inside.
"My mom sent this." / "Yes, thank you."
"Goodbye." / "Okay. Goodbye."

Classwork and Homework

1. Follow the model shown. Fill in the blanks using the words on the left.

   1) 아주머니 계세요?

      A) Grandfather | | 아 | | | 계 | | | ?

      B) Someone (Hint: who) | | | | | | ?

   2) 어머니가 이것을 보내셨어요.

      A) Father, book | | | | | | | | 보내셨어요.

      B) Teacher, sent | | | | 메모를 | | | | | | .

      C) Grandmom, rice cake | | | | | | | 보내셨어요.

2. What expressions can you use in the following situations?

   1) Someone gave you a gift. | | | | | | .

   2) Your dad helped you with homework. | | | | | .

3. Describe a situation in which you might use these expressions.

   ◆ 실례합니다.   ◆ 미안합니다.

Let's Eat!

Boy, I am starved! After a long day at school, I get so hungry that I could eat a horse! Let's eat!

10. 식사 I (Meal I)

식사 시간입니다.

우리는 밥과 국을 먹습니다.

김치, 찌개, 맛있는 반찬을 먹습니다.

나는 불고기를 좋아합니다.

No, I don't really eat horses. It's just an old saying.

But I do like meat! Hee hee.

New Vocabulary

식사 시간 mealtime	밥 rice, meal
국 soup	먹습니다(먹다) to eat
김치 kimchi	찌개 stew
맛있는 delicious	반찬 side dish
불고기 *bulgogi*	좋아합니다(좋아하다) to like

1. Present Tense Verb Forms [Part 1]

In Korean, there are three basic verb forms.

Note: The first two forms are usually used in writing, while the third is used most often in conversation.

Dictionary Form	Plain -ㄴ다 Form	Moderate/Formal -ㅂ니다 Form	Casual -요 Form
가다 to go	간다	갑니다	가요
먹다 to eat	먹는다	먹습니다	먹어요

2. How to Make These Verb Forms

Step 1: Verb stem.

1) Get the verb stem. Find the dictionary form and take away 다.
   Ex. Dictionary Form: 가다 — 다 = Verb Stem: 가.

Step 2: For verbs with no final consonant, just add the verb stem and the ending.

2) Verb stems with <u>no final consonant</u>:
   Ex. 가다 (verb stem 가)

–ㄴ다 form:	**verb stem +** ㄴ다	가다 → 간다
–ㅂ니다) form:	**verb stem +** ㅂ니다	가다 → 갑니다
–요 form:	**verb stem +** 요	가다 → 가요

For verbs with a final consonant, read the rules carefully.

3) Verb stems with a <u>final consonant</u>:
   Ex. 먹다 (verb stem 먹)

–ㄴ다 form:	**verb stem +** 는다	먹다 → 먹는다
–ㅂ니다) form:	**verb stem +** 습니다	먹다 → 먹습니다
–요 form:	**verb stem +** 아요*	좋다 → 좋아요
	verb stem + 어요*	먹다 → 먹어요

*Note: Add 아요 if the final vowel in the verb stem is either ㅏ or ㅗ; add 어요 if the final vowel in the verb stem is ㅓ, ㅜ, ㅡ, or ㅣ.

Translation

It is mealtime. We eat rice and soup. Also, we eat kimchi, stew, and delicious side dishes. I like bulgogi.

Classwork and Homework

1. Fill in the blanks to form the sentence on the left.

    1) I eat rice.

    나 는 　 을 　 　 .

    2) My sister eats kimchi.

    　 　 　 를 　 .

    3) We eat bulgogi.

    　 는 　 　 먹 요 .

2. Change the verb form from moderate to <u>casual</u>.

    1) 나는 먹습니다.　　→　나는 　 　 .

    2) 아빠는 이를 닦습니다.　→　아빠는 이를 　 　 .

    3) 어머니는 옷을 입습니다. →　어머니는 옷을 　 　 .

3. Change the verbal form from moderate to <u>plain</u>.

    1) 나는 먹습니다.　　→　나는 　 　 .

    2) 아빠는 이를 닦습니다.　→　아빠는 이를 　 　 .

    3) 어머니는 옷을 입습니다. →　어머니는 옷을 　 　 .

4. Ask your teacher or your mom about the following foods.

    잡채, 만두, 자장면, 국수, 갈비, 냉면, 비빔밥

Let's Learn about the Four Seasons!

It's time to go outside and play again! I wish it was summer because then we could go swimming. We could eat lots of ice cream, too. What's your favorite season?

II. 사계절 (Four Seasons)

봄, 여름, 가을, 겨울.

봄에는 새싹이 나옵니다.

여름에는 나무가 자랍니다.

가을에는 열매가 익습니다.

겨울에는 눈이 내립니다.

New Vocabulary

봄 spring	여름 summer
가을 fall	겨울 winter
새싹 bud	나옵니다(나오다) to come out
나무 tree	자랍니다(자라다) to grow
열매 fruit (of a tree)	익습니다(익다) to ripen
눈 snow	내립니다(내리다) to come down; to fall

Grammar and Notes

Grammar

Present Tense Verb Forms [Part 2]

Let's review what we learned last time.

	Dict. Form	Verb Stem	–ㄴ다	–ㅂ니다	–(아/어)요
W/O Final Con.	자다 to sleep	자–	잔다	잡니다	자요
	가다 to go	가–	간다	갑니다	가요
W/ Final Con.	닦다 to brush (teeth)	닦–	닦는다	닦습니다	닦아요
	먹다 to eat	먹–	먹는다	먹습니다	먹어요
	빗다 to brush (hair)	빗–	빗는다	빗습니다	빗어요

Some verbs don't exactly follow the pattern above. Note the changes and memorize the following chart of commonly used verbs and the present tense forms.

Reminder: The form of the verb does not change because of *number* (singular/plural) or *person*. (I, you, he/she/it). ie. 먹는다 can mean *I eat, you eat, he eats*, etc.

Dict. Form	Verb Stem	–ㄴ다	–ㅂ니다	–요
하다 to do	하–	한다	합니다	해요
오다 to come	오–	온다	옵니다	와요
살다 to live	살–	산다	삽니다	살아요
있다 there is	있–	있다	있습니다	있어요

Translation

Spring, summer, fall, winter. In the spring, buds come out. In the summer, trees grow. In the fall, fruits ripen. In the winter, snow falls.

54

Classwork and Homework

1. Match the phrases together to form the sentence on the right.

봄에는 ○   ○ 열매가 익는다. *In the fall, fruits ripen.*

여름에는 ○   ○ 새싹이 나온다. *In the spring , buds come out.*

가을에는 ○   ○ 눈이 내린다. *In the winter, snow falls.*

겨울에는 ○   ○ 나무가 자란다. *In the summer, trees grow.*

2. Change the verb form from plain to <u>casual</u>.

   1) 열매가 익는다. → ☐☐☐ ☐☐☐ .

   2) 새싹이 나온다. → ☐☐☐ ☐☐☐ .

   3) 눈이 내린다. → ☐☐ ☐☐☐ .

   4) 나무가 자란다. → ☐☐☐ ☐☐☐ .

3. Name the season you see in the picture below.

  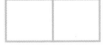 

Let's Say Bye to My Sister!

My sister is going on a trip tomorrow. She is going camping in the woods with her friend's family. She's packing her clothes right now.

12. 옷 (Clothes)

내일 누나는 캠핑을 갑니다.
누나 혼자서 물건을 준비합니다.
청바지, 티셔츠, 속옷, 양말 등을
가방에 넣습니다.

Yay! I'm glad she's going away. Now, I can do whatever
I want by myself. . . and with you, of course!

New Vocabulary

내일 tomorrow	캠핑 camping
혼자서 by oneself, alone	물건 things
준비합니다(준비하다) to prepare	청바지 jeans
티셔츠 T-shirt	속옷 undergarments
양말 socks	등 etc.
가방 bag	넣습니다(넣다) to put into

Grammar and Notes

Vocabulary

Things to Wear

구두 dress shoes	모자 hat	바지 pants
벨트 belt	블라우스 blouse	속옷 underwear
스웨터 sweater	신발 shoes	안경 glasses
양복 suit	운동화 sneakers	재킷 jacket
치마 skirt	티셔츠 T-shirt	반바지 shorts
셔츠 shirt	양말 socks	청바지 jeans

Phrase

Expressions to Mean "to Wear" or "to Put on"
신다, 쓰다, 끼다 and 입다

These four different verbs all mean "to wear" or "to put on."

1) 신다 for shoes and socks
   누나는 양말을 __신어요__. *My sister wears socks.*
   아빠는 구두를 __신어요__. *Dad puts on shoes.*

2) 쓰다 for hats and glasses
   친구는 모자를 __써요__. *My friend wears a hat.*
   할아버지는 안경을 __써요__. *Grandpa puts on glasses.*

3) 끼다 for rings and gloves
   엄마는 반지를 __껴요__. *Mom wears a ring.*
   누나는 장갑을 __껴요__. *My sister puts on gloves.*

4) 입다 for all other articles of clothing
   엄마는 치마를 __입어요__. *Mom wears the dress.*
   나는 바지를 __입어요__. *I put on pants.*

Translation

Tomorrow, my sister is going camping. She prepares her things herself. She puts jeans, a T-shirt, undergarments, socks, etc. into her bag.

Classwork and Homework

1. What other equipments do you need for camping? Discuss it in class and write down some of them in Korean.

2. Use these words to fill in the blanks: 신어요, 써요, 입어요 and 껴요.

   1) 아빠는 모자를 [ ][ ].

   2) 나는 바지를 [ ][ ][ ].

   3) 누나는 속옷을 [ ][ ].

   4) 할머니는 양말을 [ ][ ][ ].

   5) 할아버지는 안경을 [ ][ ].

   6) 엄마는 장갑을 [ ][ ].

   7) 엄마는 구두를 [ ][ ].

   8) 누나는 반지를 [ ][ ].

3. Ask these questions to your classmates and write down their answers.

   1) 아침에 무엇을 입어요?
      What do you wear in the morning?

      [ ]

   2) 아침에 무엇을 신어요?
      What do you wear in the morning?

      [ ]

Let's Learn about Korea!

I'm bored. I know what you're thinking. You think that I miss my sister. Well, I don't. I just want to go somewhere too. How about we take a trip to Korea? I read that it's very beautiful. Here, take a look.

13. 자연 (Nature)

자연은 매우 아름답습니다.

산에는 많은 나무가 자랍니다.

들에는 파란 채소가 자랍니다.

골짜기에는 맑은 물이 흐릅니다.

바다에는 큰 파도가 출렁거립니다.

Well, I guess we can't really go to Korea right now. We better think of another idea.

New Vocabulary

자연 nature	매우 very	
아름답습니다 (아름답다) to be pretty, to be beautiful		
산 mountain	많은 many	들 plain, field
파란 green	채소 vegetable	골짜기 valley
맑은 clear	물 water	흐릅니다(흐르다) to flow
바다 sea	큰 big	파도 wave
출렁거리다 to roll		

Grammar and Notes

Grammar

Reminder: To make the adjective stem, find the dictionary adjective form and take away the 다. This is just like finding the verb stem.

Adjectives

A. There are two cases of adjective usage:

1) Predicate	물이 **맑다**. The water is clear.	바다는 **깊다**. The sea is deep.	하늘이 **높다**. The sky is high.
2) Modifier	**맑은** 물 clear water	**깊은** 바다 deep sea	**높은** 하늘 high sky

B. To make the modifier form of the adjective, take the adjective stem + ㄴ.

1) 크(다) + ㄴ = 큰　　Ex. 큰 나무 *(big tree)*
2) 높(다) + ㄴ = 높은　Ex. 높은 산 *(high mountain)*
3) 파랗(다) + ㄴ = 파란　Ex. 파란 들 *(green field)*

Developing Sentences

(Basic form)	채소가 자랍니다.
(What kind?)	**파란** 채소가 자랍니다.
(Where?)	**들에는** 파란 채소가 자랍니다.
(Final sentence)	*Green vegetables grow in the field.*

Translation

Nature is very beautiful. In the mountains, many trees grow. In the field, green vegetables grow. In the valley, clear water flows. In the sea, the big waves roll.

1. Match the phrases to form a sentence.

산에는 ○   ○ 채소가 자랍니다.

골짜기에는 ○   ○ 파도가 출렁거립니다.

바다에는 ○   ○ 나무가 자랍니다.

들에는 ○   ○ 물이 흐릅니다.

2. Change the adjective to the modifier form.

Ex. 채소가 파랗다.   → | 파 | 란 | 채소

1) 파도가 크다.   → | | 파도

2) 나무가 많다.   → | | | 나무

3) 반찬이 맛있다.   → | | | | 반찬

3. What can you find or see. . .

1) in the mountains?

2) in the backyard?

3) in the park?

Let's Play with Toys!

Hey, I know! Let's go to my friend Cathy's house. She is really cool, and she has lots of cool toys that we can play with. We can play with robots and toy cars. Let's go!

14. 장난감 (Toys)

나는 캐티하고 놉니다.

나는 로봇을 가지고 놉니다.

캐티는 인형을 가지고 놉니다.

머리를 빗기고 옷을 갈아 입힙니다.

That was fun. No, I do not like Cathy. Eww. . . Well,
I think I should go home now. But I'll see you later!

New Vocabulary

로봇 robot	가지고 놉니다(놀다) to play with
인형 doll	빗기고(빗기다) to brush
입힙니다(입히다) to dress, to put … on	

Grammar and Notes

Conjunctions
…하고(*with*) and …고(*and*)

Case 1: Usage of …**하고**

　　…하고 (*with, and*) can be used like …와 / 과 …
　　to connect two words.

　　Ex. 순이**하고** 철수(순이와 철수) *Sooni and Chulsoo*
　　　　아빠**하고** 나(아빠와 나) *Dad and I*
　　　　자동차**하고** 로봇(자동차와 로봇) *The car and the robot*

Case 2: Usage of **고**

　　…고 (*and*) is used to connect two clauses.

　　Ex. 나는 머리를 빗긴다. 나는 옷을 갈아 입힌다.(2 sentences)
　　　　I comb its hair. I change its clothes.
　　　　나는 머리를 빗기**고** 옷을 갈아 입힙니다.(1 sentence)
　　　　I comb its hair and change its clothes.

　　　　나무가 자란다. 물이 흐른다.(2 sentences)
　　　　The tree grows. The water flows.
　　　　나무가 자라**고*** 물이 흐른다.(1 sentence)
　　　　The tree grows and the water flows.

*Use the conjunction -고 in the following way: Verb stem + 고
　　Ex. 자라다 (자라 - verb stem) : 자라고

Translation

I am playing with Cathy. I play with a robot. Cathy plays with a doll. She brushes its hair and changes its clothes.

1. Fill in the blanks using the expression …하고.

Ex. 나는 | 친 | 구 | 하 | 고 | 학교에 가요.   *I go to school <u>with my friend</u>.*

1) 나는 [| | |] 산에 가요.   *I go to the mountain <u>with dad</u>.*

2) 누나는 [| |] 캠핑가요.   *My sister goes camping <u>with her friend</u>.*

3) 엄마는 [| |] 시장에 가요.   *Mom goes to the market <u>with my sister</u>.*

4) 캐티는 [|] 놀아요.   *Kathy plays <u>with me</u>.*

2. Combine the two sentences into one, using the expression …고.

Ex. 나는 밥을 먹어요. 나는 놀아요.

→ 나는 밥을 먹<u>고</u> 놀아요.

1) 나무가 크다. 나무가 푸르다.

→ 나무가 [|] 푸르다.

2) 바다는 넓다. 파도가 출렁거린다.

→ 바다는 [|] 파도가 출렁거린다.

3) 우리는 공부해요. 우리는 놀아요.

→ 우리는 [| | |] 놀아요.

Let's Play Sports!

Hi! It's nice to see you again at my school. We just finished all our classes. Now it's time to play sports! Do you play any sports?

15. 운동 (Sports)

학생들이 공부를 마치고 운동을 합니다.

가을에는 축구와 풋볼,

겨울에는 농구와 수영,

봄에는 테니스와 야구를 합니다.

나는 그 중에서 수영을 가장 좋아합니다.

I like swimming the most. What's your favorite sport?

New Vocabulary

학생 pupil, student	마치고(마치다) to finish
운동 sports	축구 soccer
풋볼 football	농구 basketball
수영 swimming	테니스 tennis
야구 baseball	그 중에서 among them
가장 the most	

Grammar and Notes

Vocabulary

Sports

골프	golf	등산	climbing	마라톤	marathon
배구	volleyball	탁구	ping-pong	태권도	taekwondo

Phrase

Expressions about Sports

When you say "to play (a sport)," use the verb 합니다 (to do), not 놉니다 (*to play*).

    Ex. 축구를 합니다. *I play soccer.*
        수영을 합니다. *I swim.*
        야구를 합니다. *I play baseball.*

Developing Sentences

1) You see the same subject in both sentences below.

   학생들이 공부를 마친다. 학생들이 운동을 한다.
   The students finish studying. The students play sports.

2) To make these into one sentence, first just <u>take away the subject</u> of the second sentence. You should see this:

   학생들이 공부를 마친다. 운동을 한다.

3) Now, <u>use the conjunction ···고</u> after the verb in the first sentence to combine the two into one sentence.

   학생들이 공부를 **마치고** 운동을 한다.
   The students finish studying <u>and</u> play sports.

Translation

After finishing studying, students play sports. In the fall, soccer and football; in the winter, basketball and swimming; in the spring, they play tennis and baseball. Among them, I like swimming the most.

Classwork and Homework

1. Reading Comprehension: Answer these questions about the story.

   1) 학생들이 언제 운동을 합니까?

      | | | | 마치고 (운동을 합니다).

   2) 가을에는 무슨 운동을 합니까?

      | | | (야구, 풋볼, 농구)

   3) 겨울에는 무슨 운동을 합니까?

      | | | (레슬링, 농구, 수영, 스키)

   4) 봄에는 무슨 운동을 합니까?

      | | | | (테니스, 축구, 배구)

   5) 어떤 운동이 공을 사용하지 않습니까?

      볼링, 농구, 야구, 탁구, 축구, 수영, 배구, 골프, 레슬링

2. Ask these questions to your classmates.

   1) 무슨 운동을 합니까? *What sport do you play?*

      A) 나는 축구를 합니다. *I play soccer.*

      B) 나는 수영을 합니다. *I swim.*

   2) 무슨 운동을 좋아합니까? *What sport do you like?*

      A) 나는 수영을 좋아합니다. *I like swimming.*

      B) 나는 테니스를 좋아합니다. *I like to play tennis.*

Let's Learn Numbers!

Summer is almost here. That means school is almost over. Yay! I like summer vacation because I can play a lot. But sometimes we do fun things in school too. Today, we read a funny story in class. Hee hee. Check it out!

16. 숫자 (Numbers)

아기 돼지들이 시냇물을 건넙니다.
언니 돼지가 세어 봅니다.
"하나, 둘, 셋, 넷, 다섯, 여섯,
일곱, 여덟, 아홉, 열, 열하나.
이상하다. 한 마리는 어디 갔을까?"
열두 마리 아기 돼지들은 한 마리가
없다고 야단입니다.

Get it? The oldest pig forgot to count herself. Duh!

New Vocabulary

아기 돼지 baby pig	시냇물 stream
건넙니다(건너다) to cross	언니 돼지 big sister pig
세어 봅니다(세어 보다) to count	이상하다 to be strange
어디 갔을까? Where did (it) go?	
야단입니다(야단이다) to fuss about	

Grammar and Notes

1. Number Names

1	일	8	팔	15	십오	22	이십이
2	이	9	구	16	십육	23	이십삼
3	삼	10	십	17	십칠		⋮
4	사	11	십일	18	십팔	30	삼십
5	오	12	십이	19	십구	31	삼십일
6	육	13	십삼	20	이십		⋮
7	칠	14	십사	21	이십일	100	백

2. Counting Numbers

One	하나	Nine	아홉	Forty	마흔
Two	둘	Ten	열	Fifty	쉰
Three	셋	Eleven	열하나	Sixty	예순
Four	넷	Twelve	열둘	Seventy	일흔
Five	다섯	Twenty	스물	Eighty	여든
Six	여섯	Twenty-one	스물하나	Ninety	아흔
Seven	일곱	Twenty-two	스물둘	Hundred	백
Eight	여덟	Thirty	서른		

Note: To count things, books, sheets of paper, dishes of food, etc. use these words:

개 thing
권 book
장 sheet of paper
그릇 dish of food

3. Counting Objects

When you say the names of the objects as you count, a few numbers (1-4, 20) are different; the rest are the same as above.

General form: 한 ( ), 두 ( ), 세 ( ), 네 ( ), 스무 ( ), etc.

> Ex. To count people, use the general form and the appropriate word: 한 사람, 두 사람, 세 사람, 네 사람, 스무 사람, etc.

The baby pigs cross the stream. The big sister pig counts them. "One, two, three, four, five, six, seven, eight, nine, ten, eleven. That's strange. Where did one go?" The twelve baby pigs fuss that the one pig is not there.

1. Reading Comprehension: Answer these questions about the story.

   1) 아기 돼지들이 무엇을 건넙니까?

   ☐☐☐ (시냇물, 강, 들)

   2) 아기 돼지들이 왜 야단을 했습니까?

   A) 배가 고파서 *because they were hungry*

   B) 길을 몰라서 *because they were lost*

   C) 한 마리가 없다고 *that there was one missing*

2. Fill in the blanks with the correct number.

   하나, 둘, ☐, 넷, ☐☐, 여섯,

   ☐☐, 여덟, ☐☐, 열, ☐☐☐

3. Count how many are in the picture and write down the answer.

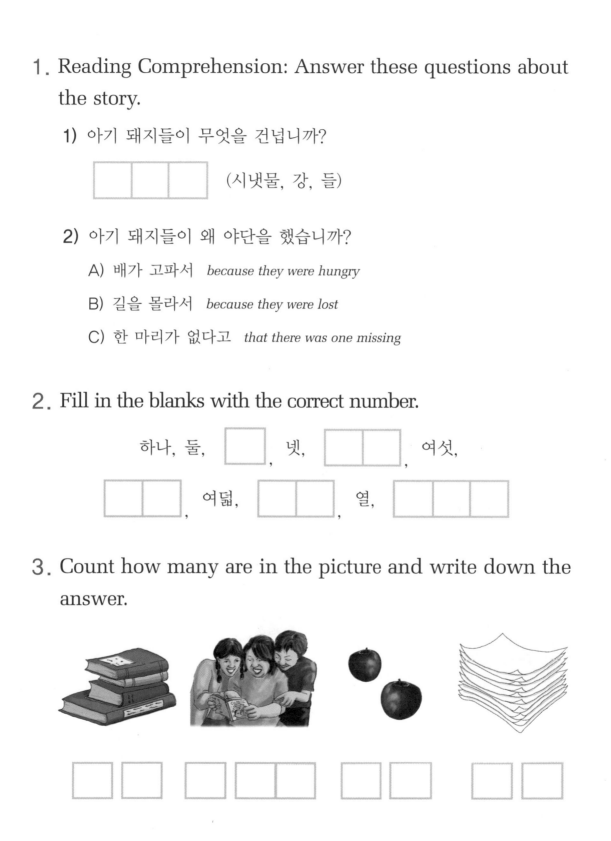

☐☐ ☐☐☐ ☐☐ ☐☐☐

Let's Learn the Colors of the Rainbow!

In the summer, there are a lot of rain showers. The rain pours down. Sometimes, there's really bright lightning and loud thunder, too. But I don't get scared because I'm a big boy. . . yikes! What was that noise?

17. 색깔 (Colors)

소나기가 온 뒤
맑은 하늘에 무지개가 보인다.

빨간색, 노란색, 파란색, 초록색, 보라색
무슨 색이 더 있을까?

아무리 살펴봐도
흰색과 검은색은 보이지 않는다.

After a shower, sometimes you can see a colorful rainbow in the sky. It's pretty, isn't it?

New Vocabulary

소나기 rain shower	온 뒤 after	하늘 sky
무지개 rainbow	보인다 to be seen; to appear	
무슨 what	더 more	있을까? is there?
아무리 no matter	살펴봐도(살펴보다) to look for	

Grammar and Notes

Vocabulary

1. Colors

In Korean, there are three basic verb forms.

	Red	Black	Yellow	Green	White	Blue
Predicate Form	빨갛다	검다	노랗다	푸르다	희다	파랗다
Modifier Form	빨간	검은	노란	푸른	흰	파란

2. Examples of Usage

Predicate Form	Modifier Form

1) 사과가 빨갛다. *The apple is red.* 빨간 사과 *the red apple*
2) 눈이 하얗다. *The snow is white.* 하얀 눈 *the white snow*
3) 풀이 푸르다. *The grass is green.* 푸른 풀 *the green grass*

3. Drill

빨간색 (red)   검은색 (black)

노란색 (yellow)   흰색 (white)

파란색 (blue)   분홍색 (pink)

보라색 (violet)   초록색 (green)

Translation

After the rain shower comes, a rainbow appears in the clear sky.
Red, yellow, blue, green, violet / What other color is there?
No matter how much we look / White and black can't be seen.

1. Reading Comprehension: Answer these questions about the story.

   1) 하늘에는 무엇이 보입니까?

      가 보입니다.

   2) 언제 무지개가 하늘에 나타났습니까?

      가 온 뒤에 (나타났어요).

   3) 무지개에서 무슨 색을 찾을 수 없습니까?

      과

2. Match the names of the colors corresponding with each other.

   빨간색 ⊙   ⊙ violet

   노란색 ⊙   ⊙ blue

   보라색 ⊙   ⊙ red

   파란색 ⊙   ⊙ yellow

3. Can you name the seven colors of the rainbow?

Let's Play the Piano!

Yesterday, I got into trouble. I was running around in the house again. This time, I tripped and broke a vase. It was my mom's favorite vase. So, now I have to try to be a really good boy. Today, I have to practice piano as my mom told me to. I better go practice now.

18. 피아노 연습 (Piano Practice)

오늘은 피아노 선생님께서 오십니다.

나는 피아노 레슨을 받습니다.

하얀 건반 위에서 손가락이 바쁘게
움직입니다.

아름다운 피아노 소리가 울립니다.

나는 피아노 연습을 열심히 합니다.

New Vocabulary

피아노 piano	오십니다(오다) to come
레슨 lesson	받습니다(받다) to take, to receive
건반 key board	위에서 on, on top of
손가락 finger	움직입니다(움직이다) to move
소리 sound	울립니다(울리다) to ring, to sound
연습 practice	열심히 hard

Grammar and Notes

Adverbs

1) Examples of Adverb Usage

사람들이 **열심히** 일해요. *People work hard.*

사람들이 **바쁘게** 다녀요. *People travel busily.*

아기는 **조용히** 놀아요. *The baby plays quietly.*

2) How to Make the Regular Adverb Form

An adverb is formed by taking an adjective stem + 게 or 히.

Ex.	Adj. form	Adj. form		Adverb
	조용하다	조용	조용 + 히	= 조용히 quietly
	바쁘다	바쁘	바쁘 + 게	= 바쁘게 busily
	열심이다	열심	열심 + 히	= 열심히 hard

3) Some Other Forms of Adverbs

김치가 **너무** 매워요. *The kimchi is too spicy.*

나는 수영이 **가장** 좋아요. *I like swimming the most.*

Developing Sentences

(Basic Form) 손가락이 움직입니다. *Fingers move.*

(Where?) 손가락이 **건반 위에서** 바쁘게 움직입니다.

(What kind?) **하얀** 건반 위에서 손가락이 바쁘게 움직입니다.

(Final Sent.) *Fingers move busily on the white keyboard.*

Translation

Today, the piano teacher is coming. I take a piano lesson. My fingers move busily on the white keyboard. The beautiful piano sound rings. I practice the piano hard.

Classwork and Homework

1. Reading Comprehension: Answer these questions about the story.

   1) 오늘 누가 오십니까?

      ☐☐☐ 선생님 (이 오십니다).

   2) 코리는 피아노 연습을 어떻게 합니까?

      ☐☐☐ 합니다.

   3) 손가락이 건반 위에서 어떻게 움직입니까?

      ☐☐☐ 움직입니다.

2. Change the adjectives to the adverb form.

   1) 바쁘다 → ☐☐☐

   2) 맛있다 → ☐ 게

   3) 아름답다 → ☐☐☐

Let's Clean the Kitchen!

My mom is still upset with me about the vase. What else can I do to get on her good side? I know! I can help clean the house. I'll start with the kitchen.

19. 부엌 (Kitchen)

우리 부엌은 늘 깨끗합니다.

식사를 한 후, 어머니께서 그릇을 깨끗이
씻으십니다.

수납장에는 접시, 컵, 냄비가 있고,

서랍에는 수저, 포크, 나이프가 있습니다.

냉장고에는 맛있는 음식이 있습니다.

Aw shux! There's nothing to clean because my mom does such a good job. Oh well . . . at least I tried. I should just stick to what I do best. Time to go play!

New Vocabulary

부엌 kitchen	늘 always	음식 food
깨끗합니다(깨끗하다) to be clean		…한 후 after
그릇 dishes	씻으십니다(씻다) to wash	
수납장 cabinet	접시 plate	컵 cup
냄비 pan	서랍 drawer	수저 spoon & chopsticks
냉장고 refrigerator	맛있는(맛있다) to be delicious	

Grammar and Notes

Phrase

1. ···한 후(에) (= ···한 다음) *after*

1) 식사를 **한 후**, 나는 이를 닦아요.
   (= 식사를 **한 다음**, 나는 이를 닦아요.)
   After having a meal, I brush my teeth.

2) 운동을 **한 후**, 나는 샤워를 해요.
   After playing sports, I take a shower.

3) 학교를 **마친 후**, 나는 집으로 와요.
   After finishing school, I come home.

2. ···하기 전(에) *before*

1) 식사를 **하기 전**, 나는 손을 씻어요.
   Before having a meal, I wash my hands.

2) **잠자기 전**, 나는 이를 닦아요.
   Before sleeping, I brush my teeth.

3) **외출하기 전**, 옷을 갈아입어요.
   Before going out, I change clothes.

Developing Sentences

(Basic Form) 어머니는 씻으십니다. *Mom washes.*

(What?)   어머니는 **그릇을** 씻으십니다.

(How?)   어머니는 그릇을 **깨끗이** 씻으십니다.

(When?)   **식사를 한 후**, 어머니는 그릇을 깨끗이 씻으십니다.

(Final Sent.) *After having a meal, Mom always washes the dishes clean.*

Translation

Our kitchen is always clean. After having a meal, mom washes the dishes. In the cabinet there is a plate, a cup, and a pan, and in the drawer there is a spoon and chopsticks, a fork, and a knife. In the refrigerator, there is delicious food.

Classwork and Homework

1. Reading Comprehension: Answer these questions about the story.

　　1) 식사를 한 후 어머니는 무엇을 합니까? *What does the mother do after a meal?*

　　　　[　|　] 을 씻어요.

　　2) 수납장에는 무엇이 있습니까? *What things are in the cabinet?*

　　　　[　|　] [　|　] [　|　] 가 있어요.

　　3) 서랍에는 무엇이 있습니까? *What things are in the drawer?*

　　　　[　|　] [　|　] [　|　|　] 가 있어요.

　　4) 냉장고에는 무엇이 있어요? *What is in the refrigerator?*

　　　　[　|　|　] 음식이 있어요.

2. Match the phrases together to form a complete sentence.

　　　식사를 한 후(에) ○　　　　○ 샤워를 해요.

　　　운동을 한 후(에) ○　　　　○ 손을 씻어요.

　　　식사를 하기 전(에) ○　　　　○ 이를 닦아요.

Let's Go Downtown!

Hey! Do you want to take a trip? We won't go too far away. We'll just take the subway and go downtown. I'm not allowed to go by myself, so usually I have to go with my older sister. But since you're here, we can just go together! Ok? Let's go!

20. 시내 (Downtown)

시내는 매우 복잡합니다.

차도에는 버스, 택시, 자동차가 다니고,

인도에는 사람들이 바쁘게 다닙니다.

높은 건물에는 상점들과 사무실이 있습니다.

시내에 갈 때, 지하철을 타면 편리합니다.

Whew, it is really busy downtown. It sure is fun to go there, but I don't think I could live there.

New Vocabulary

시내 downtown	매우 very
복잡합니다 (복잡하다) to be busy	차도 roadway
버스 bus	택시 taxi
자동차 automobile	다니고 (다니다) to travel
인도 sidewalk	바쁘게 busily
높은 건물 high-rise buildings	상점 shop
사무실 office	…할 때 when
지하철 subway	타면 (타다) to ride, to take
편리합니다 (편리하다) to be convenient	

Grammar and Notes

Phrase

1. ···때 (*when*)

1) 시내에 가다 → 시내에 갈 <u>때</u> <u>when you go downtown</u>
2) 운동을 하다 → 운동을 할 <u>때</u> <u>when you play sports</u>
3) 공부를 하다 → 공부를 할 <u>때</u> <u>when you study</u>

2. ···면 (*if*)

1) 지하철을 타다 → 지하철을 타<u>면</u> if you take the subway
2) 운동을 하다 → 운동을 하<u>면</u> if you play sports
3) 공부를 하다 → 공부를 하<u>면</u> if you study

Grammar

Plural, ···들

How to Make the Plural Form: Just add 들 to the singular noun.

Singular Noun	Plural Noun
상점 *store*	상점<u>들</u> *stores*
차 *car*	차<u>들</u> *cars*
아이 *child*	아이<u>들</u> *children*

Remember: There is no change in the verb form because of changes in person or number.

Singular Subject	Plural Subject
사람이 **있습니다.** *There is a person.*	사람들이 **있습니다.** *There are people.*
차가 **다닙니다.** *A car travels.*	차들이 **다닙니다.** *Cars travel.*

Translation

Downtown is very busy. On the roadways, buses, taxis, and cars travel, and on the sidewalk people move busily. In the high-rise buildings, there are shops and offices. When you go downtown, it is convenient if you take the subway.

1. Reading Comprehension: Answer these questions about the story.

   1) 시내는 얼마나 복잡합니까?

      □□ 복잡해요.

   2) 높은 건물에는 무엇이 있습니까?

      □□ 과 □□□ 이 있어요.

   3) 시내에 갈 때 무엇을 타면 편리합니까?

      □□□ 을 타면 편리해요.

2. Change the sentence to a when-clause using the …때 phrase.

   1) 식사를 한다. → 식사를 □□

   2) 학교에 간다. → □□ 에 □ □

   3) 여름이 온다. → □□ 이 □ □

3. Change the sentence to an if-clause using the …면 phrase.

   1) 운동을 하다 → 운동을 □□

   2) 공부를 하다 → 공부를 □□

4. Change the words from singular to plural form.

   1) 사람 □□□   2) 상점 □□□   3) 차 □□

Let's Look around My Neighborhood!

Did you have fun on our trip downtown? I actually like my neighborhood better. It's quiet and clean. Also, there are a lot of places to run around and play. You know how much I like to run around! Come on. I'll show you around.

21. 동네 (Community)

우리 동네는 살기에 참 좋습니다.

조용하고 아름답습니다.

호숫가에는 조용한 산책길이 있습니다.

학교와 병원과 도서관이 있습니다.

집 가까이에 시장이 있기 때문에 편리합니다.

New Vocabulary

동네 community, neighborhood	살기에(살다) to live
좋습니다(좋다) to be good	참 very
조용하고(조용하다) to be quiet	호숫가 lakefront
산책길 path	병원 hospital
도서관 library	가까이 near
편리합니다(편리하다) to be convenient	시장 market

Grammar and Notes

Phrase

…때문에 (*because*)

1) 아프기 **때문에** 학교에 못 가요.
   Because I am sick, I cannot go to school.

2) 덥기 **때문에** 수영을 해요. *Because it is hot, I swim.*

3) 배고프기 **때문에** 먹어요. *Because I am hungry, I eat.*

Developing Sentences

1) (Basic Form)   동네는 좋습니다. *The neighborhood is good.*
   (Whose?)   **우리** 동네는 좋습니다.
   (How good?)   우리 동네는 **참** 좋습니다.
   (Why?)   우리 동네는 **살기에** 참 좋습니다.
   (Final sent.) *Our neighborhood is very good to live in.*

2) (Basic Form)   **편리합니다.** *It is convenient.*
   (Why?)   **시장이 있기 때문에** 편리합니다.
   (Where?)   **집 가까이** 시장이 있기 때문에 편리합니다.
   (Final sent.) *Because there is a market near my house, it is convenient.*

Oral Drill

왜 (   )을/를 합니까?

Teacher: **왜** 운동을 합니까? *Why do you play sports?*
Student: 재미있기 **때문에** 운동을 합니다.
    I play sports because it is fun.

Translation

Our neighborhood is very good to live in. It is quiet and beautiful. There is a quiet path by the lake. There is a school, a hospital, and a library. It is convenient because there is a market near my house.

Classwork and Homework

1. Reading Comprehension: Answer these questions about the story.

   1) 코리의 동네는 어떻습니까?

   [ ][ ][ ] 좋습니다.

   2) 호숫가에는 무엇이 있습니까?

   [ ][ ][ ] 이 있습니다.

   3) 집 가까이 무엇이 있습니까?

   [ ][ ] 이 있습니다.

2. Fill in the blank with the correct conjunction, 와 or 과.

   1) 시장 [ ] 집   2) 학교 [ ] 호수

   3) 도서관 [ ] 병원   4) 상점 [ ] 사무실

3. Answer the questions using the verbs given below.

   1) 왜 학교에 못 갑니까? *Why can't you go to school?* (아프다)

   [ ][ ] 기 때문에 학교에 못 가요.

   2) 왜 수영을 합니까? *Why do you swim?* (덥다)

   [ ][ ] 때문에 수영을 해요.

Let's Buy School Supplies!

Well, that sad time of year has come again. Summer vacation is almost over. It's time to go back to school. I better start getting ready for school. Today, I'm going to buy school supplies.

22. 학용품 (School Supplies)

방학이 거의 끝났습니다.

나는 학교 갈 준비를 시작했습니다.

학용품을 사기 위해서 문구점으로 갔습니다.

공책, 연필, 지우개, 종이를 샀습니다.

어머니께서 책가방을 새로 사 주셨습니다.

Actually, going back to school is not so bad. I got to buy lots of new things like cool folders. I'm going to go draw with my new crayons now. Bye.

New Vocabulary

방학 vacation	거의 almost
끝났다(끝나다) to end	갈 준비 preparation to go
시작했다(시작하다) to start	사기 위해서 in order to buy
문구점 stationery store	연필 pencil
지우개 eraser	종이 paper
샀다(사다) to buy	책가방 backpack
새로 newly	사 주셨다(사 주다) to buy for

Grammar and Notes

Phrase

···하기 위해서 (*in order to*)

1) 나는 **공부하기 위해서** 도서관에 갔다.
   I went to the library in order to study.

2) 엄마는 물건을 **사기 위해서** 시장에 갔다.
   Mom went to the market to buy things.

3) 나는 학용품을 **사기 위해서** 문구점으로 갔어요.
   I went to the stationery store in order to buy school supplies.

Grammar

Past Tense Verb Forms [Part 1]

Note: The first two forms are usually used in writing, while the third is used most often in conversation.

*Notice that the past tense is always marked by the final consonant ㅆ.

Present form	Past form
나는 간다. *I go.*	나는 갔다. *I went.*

Just as in the present tense, there are three verb forms.

Dict. Form	Plain (–ㅆ다).	Moderate / Formal (–ㅆ습니다)	Casual (–ㅆ어요)
하다 *to do*	했다	했습니다	했어요
사다 *to buy*	샀다	샀습니다	샀어요

Developing Sentences

(Basic form) 나는 갔다. *I went.*

(To where?) 나는 **문구점으로** 갔어요.

(Why?) 나는 **학용품을 사기 위해서** 문구점으로 갔어요.

(Final sent.) *I went to the stationery store to buy school supplies.*

Translation

Vacation is almost over. I have begun to prepare to go to school. I went to the stationery store in order to buy school supplies. We bought notebooks, pencils, erasers, and paper. Mom bought a new backpack for me.

Classwork and Homework

1. Reading Comprehension: Answer these questions about the story.

   1) 무엇이 거의 끝났습니까?

   ☐☐ 이 거의 끝났어요.

   2) 코리는 왜 문구점으로 갔습니까?

   학용품을 ☐☐ ☐☐☐ 갔어요.

   3) 책가방은 누가 사 주셨습니까?

   ☐☐☐ 께서 사 주셨어요.

2. Change the sentences from the present tense to the past tense.

   1) 나는 학교에 간다.   →   나는 학교에 ☐☐.

   2) 누나는 노트를 산다.   →   누나는 노트를 ☐☐.

   3) 우리는 운동을 한다.   →   우리는 운동을 ☐☐.

3. Fill in the blanks using the ···하기 위해서 phrase.

   1) 왜 학교에 갔습니까?

   공부 ☐☐ ☐☐☐ 학교에 갔어요.

   2) 왜 시장에 갔습니까?

   물건을 ☐☐ ☐☐☐ 시장에 갔어요.

Let's Go Buy Some Food at the Store!

Hey, there! My mom is going to the store today to buy some food. I'm going with her to help out. Maybe she'll let me push the cart. Or maybe she'll let me ride in the cart! Sometimes, she buys candy and other yummy treats. Come on, let's go!

23. 과일 (Fruit)

나는 어머니를 따라 시장에 갔습니다.

과일 상점에는 사과, 수박, 딸기, 포도,

바나나 등이 가득 쌓여 있었고,

채소 시장에는 오이, 감자, 배추, 파 등

싱싱한 야채들이 있었습니다.

어머니는 딸기와 몇 가지 야채를 사셨습니다.

Phooey. She bought some strawberries and vegetables. Yuk!
I don't like vegetables. Who likes vegetables? I think we
should only eat meat all the time. Bulgogi . . . mmm.

New Vocabulary

사과 apple	수박 watermelon	딸기 strawberry
포도 grape	바나나 banana	가득 full
쌓여 있고(쌓이다) to be piled up		채소 vegetable
오이 cucumber	감자 potato	배추 cabbage
파 green onion	싱싱한 fresh	야채 vegetable
몇 가지 several		

Grammar and Notes

Grammar

Past Tense Verb Forms [Part 2]

How to Make Past Tense Verb Forms. General Rule.

Verb stem + (았, 었, or 였) + Ending form (다, 습니다, or 어요)

1) If the verb stem ends in the vowels ㅏ or ㅗ, add 았 to the ending form.

Note: Notice the contraction from: 가(았)다 to 갔다

Dict. Form	–ㅆ다 Ending	–ㅆ습니다 Ending	–ㅆ어요 Ending
가다 *to go* 보다 *to see* 살다 *to live*	가(았)다 → 갔다 보(았)다 → 보았다 살(았)다 → 살았다	갔습니다 보았습니다 살았습니다	갔어요 보았어요 살았어요

2) If the verb stem ends in the vowels ㅓ, ㅜ, ㅡ, or ㅣ, add 었 to the ending form.

Dict. Form	–었다 Ending	–었습니다 Ending	–었어요 Ending
없다 *there is no* 있다 *there is* 먹다 *to eat*	없(었)다 → 없었다 있(었)다 → 있었다 먹(었)다 → 먹었다	없었습니다 있었습니다 먹었습니다	없었어요 있었어요 먹었어요

*The ending form is contracted, so just add 했다, 했습니다 and 했어요 to the verb stem.

3) If the verb ends in 하다, add 였 to the ending form*.

Dict. Form	–였다	–였습니다	–였어요
공부하다 *to study*	공부하(였다)	공부했습니다	공부했어요

Translation

I followed mom to the market. In the fruit store, apples, water-melons, strawberries, grapes, bananas, etc. were piled up high, and in the vegetable market there were fresh vegetables: cucumbers, potatoes, cabbages, green onions, etc.
Mom bought strawberries and several vegetables.

Classwork and Homework

1. Reading Comprehension: Answer these questions about the story.

   1) 코리는 누구를 따라 시장에 갔습니까?

   ☐☐☐ 를 ☐☐ 시장에 갔어요.

   2) 과일 상점에는 무슨 과일이 가득 쌓여 있었습니까?

   ☐☐ , ☐☐ , ☐☐ , ☐☐ ,

   ☐☐ 등이 가득 쌓여 있었어요.

   3) 채소 시장에는 무슨 야채들이 있었습니까?

   ☐☐ , ☐☐ , ☐ , ☐☐ 가 있었어요.

2. Match the present tense verb form with its past tense form.

   간다 ○   ○ 샀어요

   먹는다 ○   ○ 있었어요

   있다 ○   ○ 갔어요

   산다 ○   ○ 먹었어요

3. Change the sentences into the <u>past tense form</u>.

   1) 시장에는 배추가 있습니다.

   시장에는 배추가 ☐☐☐☐☐ .

   2) 어머니는 야채를 삽니다.

   어머니는 야채를 ☐☐☐ .

Let's Read a Story!

Sorry, I can't play right now. I have to finish my homework. Now that school has started, I can't play whenever I want. The teacher gave me a lot of things to read. Maybe you can help me out. Can you let me know what it says?

24. 토끼와 거북이 (Tortoise & Hare)

토끼와 거북이가 경주를 합니다.

토끼는 빠릅니다.

토끼는 거북이보다 빨리 뛰어갑니다.

거북이는 느리지만, 쉬지 않고 기어갑니다.

토끼가 잠든 사이에, 쉬지 않고 기어간

거북이가 이겼습니다.

Thanks for your help. I think I'm finished my homework now.

New Vocabulary

토끼 hare, rabbit	거북이 tortoise, turtle
경주 race	빠릅니다(빠르다) to be fast
…보다 … than (compared to)	뛰어갑니다(뛰어가다) to run
느리지만(느리다) to be slow	쉬지 않고 without resting
기어갑니다(기어가다) to crawl	잠든(잠들다) to fall asleep
… 사이에 during, while	이겼습니다(이기다) to win

Grammar and Notes

1. …보다 더 (*more than*)

1) 토끼는 거북이**보다 더** 빨라요.
   The hare is faster than the tortoise.

2) 기차는 버스**보다 더** 빨라요. *A train is faster than a bus.*

3) 형은 나**보다 더** 커요. *My older brother is bigger than me.*

2. …지 않고 (*without*)

1) 순이는 놀**지 않고** 공부해요. *Sooni studies without playing.*

2) 아버지는 쉬**지 않고** 일해요. *Dad works without resting.*

3) 버스가 서**지 않고** 가요. *The bus goes without stopping.*

3. …지만 (*even though*)

1) 거북이는 느리**지만**, 쉬지 않고 기어갑니다.
   Even though the tortoise is slow, it crawls without resting.

2) 춥**지만** 나는 달리기를 합니다.
   Even though it is cold, I jog.

3) 피곤하**지만** 숙제를 합니다.
   Even though I am tired, I do homework.

Developing Sentences

(Basic Form) 거북이가 이겼습니다. *The tortoise won the race.*
(Which turtle?) **쉬지 않고 기어간** 거북이가 이겼습니다.
(When?) **토끼가 잠든 사이에**, 쉬지 않고 기어간 거북이가 이겼습니다.
(Final sent.) *While the hare fell asleep, the tortoise who crawled without resting won the race.*

Translation

The tortoise and the hare race. The hare is fast. The hare runs faster than the tortoise. Even though the tortoise is slow, it crawls without resting. While the hare fell asleep, the tortoise who crawled without resting won the race.

Classwork and Homework

1. Reading Comprehension: Answer these questions about the story.

   1) 누가 경주합니까?

   ☐☐☐ 와 ☐☐ 가 경주해요.

   2) 토끼와 거북이 중 누가 더 빠릅니까?

   ☐☐ 가 더 빨라요.

   3) 거북이는 어떻게 기어갔습니까?

   ☐☐ ☐☐ 기어갔어요.

   4) 누가 경주에서 이겼습니까?

   ☐☐☐ 가 이겼어요.

2. Fill in the blanks with the appropriate expressions.

   1) 토끼는 거북이 ☐☐ ☐ 빨라요.

   The hare runs faster than the tortoise.

   2) 누나는 나 ☐☐ ☐ 커요. *My sister is taller than me.*

   3) 거북이는 쉬지 ☐☐ 기어갑니다. *The tortoise crawls without resting.*

   4) 나는 놀지 ☐☐ 공부해요. *I study without playing.*

   5) 거북이는 ☐☐☐☐ 쉬지 않고 기어갑니다.

   Even though the tortoise is slow, it crawls without resting.

Let's Find a Book at the Library!

Oh no! I forgot to do something. I have to read a whole storybook and give a report on it tomorrow. Do you know any good storybooks that I can read? Something that is short and has lots of pictures would be perfect. I better go to the library to find a book.

25. 도서관 (Library)

나는 학교 도서관에 갔습니다.

도서관에는 책이 많이 있습니다.

사전, 전기, 소설, 동화책, 잡지가 있습니다.

모두 소리 없이 책을 읽고 있었습니다.

아무도 이야기하는 사람이 없습니다.

나도 조용히 동화책을 읽었습니다.

New Vocabulary

도서관 library	책 book
사전 dictionary	전기 biography
소설 novel	동화책 storybook
잡지 magazine	모두 all, everyone
소리 없이 without noise/talking	없습니다(없다) there is/are no
조용히 quietly	읽었습니다(읽다) to read

Grammar and Notes

Phrase

…없이 (*without*)

1) 소리 **없이** 책을 읽어요. I read a book <u>without</u> a noise.

2) 아빠는 말 **없이** 신문을 읽어요.
   Dad reads the newspaper <u>without</u> a word.

Grammar

Negative Form [Part 1]

To change a sentence into the negative form, add 안, 없, or 못 to the verb.

1) Usage of 안 (*not*)

Ex: 나는 산에 **안** 가요. *I don't go to the mountains.*

Sentence	Negative Form
나는 산에 **가요**. 순이는 수영을 **해요**.	나는 산에 **안** 가요. 순이는 수영을 **안** 해요.

2) Usage of 못 (*cannot*)

Ex: 나는 수영을 **못** 해요. *I can't swim.*

Sentence	Negative Form
나는 수영을 **해요**. 철수는 피아노를 **쳐요**.	나는 수영을 **못** 해요. 철수는 피아노를 **못** 쳐요.

3) Usage of 없 (*there is no/not*)

Ex: 방에 사람이 **없어요**. *There are no people in the room.*

Sentence	Negative Form
방에 사람이 **있어요**. 공원에 개가 **있어요**.	방에 사람이 **없어요**. 공원에 개가 **없어요**.

Translation

I went to the school library. In the library, there are many books. There are dictionaries, biographies, novels, storybooks, and magazines. All were reading their books without noise. There was no one talking. I, too, read a storybook quietly.

Classwork and Homework

1. Reading Comprehension: Answer these questions about the story.

   1) 코리는 어디에 갔습니까?

      ☐☐☐ 에 갔어요.

   2) 도서관에는 무슨 책이 있습니까?

      ☐☐ , ☐☐ , ☐☐ , ☐☐ 책이 있어요.

   3) 도서관에서 사람들이 무엇을 하고 있습니까?

      소리 없이 ☐ 을 읽고 있어요.

   4) 코리는 무슨 책을 읽었습니까?

      ☐☐☐ 을 읽었어요.

2. Change the sentences to the negative form using 없, 안, or 못.

   1) 사람이 있어요. —there isn't→ 사람이 ☐☐☐ .

      책이 있습니다. 책이 ☐☐☐☐ .

   2) 나는 학교에 갑니다. —not→ 나는 학교에 ☐ ☐☐☐ .

      우리는 공부를 해요. 우리는 공부를 ☐ ☐ .

   3) 나는 책을 읽어요. —cannot→ 나는 책을 ☐ ☐☐ .

      코리는 수영을 해요. 코리는 수영을 ☐ ☐ .

Let's Clean up the Mess!

Look at this. This is disgusting! I'm so mad right now! People keep throwing away trash on the streets. It makes our neighborhood dirty. My dad goes out every morning to clean the neigborhood with the other neighbors. Why should they have to clean other peoples' mess? I went to help my dad this morning. I'm a good boy, aren't I?

26. 청소 (Cleaning)

아버지께서 매일 아침 골목 청소를 하십니다.

오늘은 나도 따라 나갔습니다.

이웃집 아저씨도 나오셨습니다.

골목이 종이, 빈 깡통, 낙엽 때문에

지저분했습니다.

모두 웃으면서 청소했습니다.

Oops. Hee hee . . . I guess I forgot that I threw out an empty can in the alley yesterday. Well, at least I cleaned up, didn't I?

New Vocabulary

매일 아침 every morning	오늘 today
이웃집 아저씨 neighbor	골목 alley
빈 깡통 empty can	낙엽 fallen leaf
지저분했습니다(지저분하다) to be messy	
웃으면서(웃다) to smile, to laugh	

Grammar and Notes

Phrase

···면서 (*while, as*)

1) 모두 **웃으면서** 청소했어요. *All cleaned as they laughed.*

2) 이야기를 **나누면서** 식사를 합니다.
   They eat while they talk.

3) 우리는 **말하면서** 걸어갑니다. *We walk as we talk.*

Grammar

Personal Pronouns

Singular	Plural
나/저 I 너/당신 you 그 남자 he 그 여자 she	우리 we 너희/당신들 you 그들 they

너(you) can only be used when the speaker (I) is senior to the other person. 저(I) can only be used when the speaker (I) is junior to the other person.

Developing Sentences

(Basic Form) 아버지는 청소를 하신다. *Dad cleans.*
(What?)   아버지는 **골목** 청소를 하신다.
(When?)   아버지는 **매일 아침** 골목 청소를 하신다.
(Final sent.) *Dad cleans the alley every morning.*

Translation

Dad cleans the alley every morning. Today I also went along. The neighbors came out too. The alley was messy because of papers, empty cans, and fallen leaves. All cleaned as they laughed.

Classwork and Homework

1. Reading Comprehension: Answer these questions about the story.

   1) 아버지는 매일 아침 무엇을 합니까?

      □□ □□ 를 하세요.

   2) 골목이 왜 지저분합니까?

      □□ , □□□ , □□ 때문에 지저분해요.

   3) 오늘은 누가 더 나왔습니까?

      □ 하고 □□□ 아저씨도 나왔어요.

2. Fill in the blanks with the ···면서 phrase.

   1) 우리는 웃으 □□ 청소했어요. *We cleaned as we laughed.*

   2) 모두 이야기하 □□ 밥을 먹어요. *All eat the meal while talking.*

   3) 우리는 이야기하 □□ 걸어갔어요. *We walked as we talked.*

3. Change the words into the plural form.

   1) 너 □□   2) 아저씨 □□□□

   3) 나 □□   4) 당신 □□□

   5) 깡통 □□□   6) 낙엽 □□□

Let's Play in the Snow!

Winter's here! Woo-hoo! Look outside. There's snow! I love playing in the snow. Don't you? You can make snowmen and other funny creatures. . . .

27. 눈사람 (Snowman)

어젯밤에 눈이 내렸습니다.

온 세상이 하얗습니다.

나는 누나와 함께 눈사람을 만듭니다.

눈, 눈썹, 코, 입도 붙이고, 모자도 씌웁니다.

손이 시리지만 재미있습니다.

But the best is throwing snowballs at people, especially my sister!

New Vocabulary

어젯밤 last night	내렸습니다(내리다) to fall
온 entire, whole	세상 world
눈썹 eyebrow	붙이고(붙이다) to stick on
모자 hat	씌웁니다(씌우다) to put on
시리지만(시리다) to be cold	재미있습니다(재미있다) to be fun

Grammar and Notes

Vocabulary

Expressions for Time

Past	Now	Future
어제 yesterday	오늘 today	내일 tomorrow
작년 last year	금년 this year	내년 next year
조금 전에 not long ago	지금 now	조금 후에 in a short while
옛날에 long time ago		나중에 later

Grammar

···도 (*even, too, also, indeed*)

Use ···도 instead of subject or object particles for emphasis.

Case 1: Replace a subject particle (가, 이, 는 → 도)

1) 나는 산에 가요.
   I go to the mountain.

   나도 산에 가요.
   I, too, go to the mountain.

2) 엄마는 상점에 가요.
   Mom goes to the store.

   엄마도 상점에 가요.
   Even mom goes to the store.

Case 2: Replace an object particle (를, 을 → 도)

1) 한국어를 배워요.
   I learn Korean.

   한국어도 배워요.
   I learn Korean also.

2) 눈사람을 만들어요.
   I make a snowman.

   눈사람도 만들어요.
   I make a snowman too.

Translation

Yesterday night, snow fell. The entire world is white. Together with my sister, I make a snowman. We stick on eyes, eyebrows, a nose, and also a mouth, and we put on a hat too. Even though our hands are cold, it is fun.

Classwork and Homework

1. Reading Comprehension: Answer these questions about the story.

   1) 언제 눈이 내렸습니까?

   ☐☐☐ 에 눈이 내렸어요.

   2) 누가 눈사람을 만들었습니까?

   ☐ 하고 ☐☐ 가 눈사람을 만들었어요.

   3) 눈사람에게 무엇을 붙였습니까?

   ☐, ☐☐, ☐, ☐ 을 붙였어요.

   4) 머리에는 무엇을 씌웠습니까?

   ☐☐ 를 씌웠어요.

2. Fill in the blanks using 도 (*even, too, also*).

   1) 엄마는 시장에 가요. 나 ☐ 시장에 가요.

   Mom goes to the market. I also go to the market.

   2) 엄마는 옷을 입어요. 누나 ☐ 옷을 입어요.

   Mom puts on clothes. My sister also puts on clothes.

   3) 나는 영어를 배워요. 한국어 ☐ 배워요.

   I learn English. I learn Korean too.

   4) 나는 축구를 해요. 나는 수영 ☐ 해요.

   I play soccer. I swim too.

Let's Learn the Different Months!

I got my new "Dogs" calendar yesterday! Wow, January has a picture of a golden retriever. February's picture is of a bulldog. I really like the cool pictures in there. Last year, I ripped out all the pictures and hung them in my room. But I convinced my mom that I would take care of my calendar this year. I'm just going to use the calendar to mark everyone's birthday this year.

28. 달 (Months)

벽에 새 달력이 있습니다.

1년에는 12달, 365일이 있습니다.

3월에는 엄마의 생신, 9월에는 내 생일,

11월에는 아빠의 생신이 있습니다.

나는 생신날에 동그라미표를 그렸습니다.

New Vocabulary

달력 calendar	년 year
달 month	생신, 생일 birthday
동그라미표 circle mark	그렸습니다(그리다) to draw

Grammar and Notes

Grammar

Possessive Particles, …의

1) 아빠의 생신 *dad's birthday*
2) 엄마의 생신 *mom's birthday*
3) 하늘의 별들 *the stars of the sky*
4) 식구들의 생일날 *the birthdays of family members*

Vocabulary

Months and Dates

1월(일월) Jan.	2월(이월) Feb.	3월(삼월) Mar.	4월 Apr.	5월 May	6월 Jun.
7월 Jul.	8월 Aug.	9월 Sep.	10월 Oct.	11월 Nov.	12월 Dec.

Ex. 2008년, 4월 9일
April 9, 2008

Translation

There is a new calendar on the wall. In one year, there are 12 months or 365 days. In March my mom's birthday, in September my birthday, and in November my dad's birthday. I drew a circle around each family member's birthday.

Classwork and Homework

1. Reading Comprehension: Answer these questions about the story.

   1) 어디에 달력이 있습니까?

      ☐ 에 달력이 있어요.

   2) 1년에는 몇 달이 있습니까?

      ☐☐ 달이 있어요.

   3) 1년에는 모두 몇 일이 있습니까?

      ☐☐☐ 일이 있어요.

   4) 3월에는 누구의 생일이 있습니까?

      ☐☐ 의 ☐☐ 이 있어요.

   5) 코리는 생일날에 무슨 표를 했습니까?

      ☐☐☐☐ 표를 그렸어요.

2. Fill in the blanks using the possessive particle ···의.

   1) 엄마 ☐ 생신   2) 아빠 ☐ 생신

   3) 누나 ☐ 옷   4) 할아버지 ☐ 모자

Let's Go Eat Some Yummy Food!

I wanted to go to my friend's house today. But my parents are dragging me to their friends' house for a dinner party. They're making me get all dressed up and even wear a tie. How am I supposed to eat with a tie on? Well, if I have to go, they better at least have good food there. It better be fun.

29. 식사 2 (Meal 2)

밥과 반찬이 밥상에 가득합니다.

모두 밥상에 둘러앉았습니다.

"음식이 참 맛있어요."

"밥을 조금 더 주세요."

"예, 많이 드세요."

모두 맛있게 식사를 합니다.

New Vocabulary

밥 rice, food	반찬 side dish
가득합니다(가득하다) to fill up	밥상 dining table
둘러앉았습니다(둘러앉다) to sit around	
맛있습니다(맛있다) to taste good	음식 food
조금 더 a little more	많이 a lot

Grammar and Notes

Phrase

1. 많이 (*a lot, much*)

1) 우리는 공부를 **많이** 해요. *We study a lot.*

2) 코끼리는 **많이** 먹어요. *The elephant eats a lot.*

3) **많이** 드세요. *Eat a lot.*

2. 조금 (*a little*)

1) 밥을 **조금** 더 주세요. *Could I have a little more rice?*

2) 돈이 **조금** 있어요. *I have a little money.*

3) 음식이 **조금** 남았어요. *There is a little food left over.*

Vocabulary

Mealtime Expressions

무엇이 ··· *What ...*

··· 매워요? *... is spicy?* 김치가 매워요. *The kimchi is spicy.*

··· 뜨거워요? *... is hot?* 찌개가 뜨거워요. *The stew is hot.*

··· 짜요? *... is salty?* 국이 짜요. *The soup is salty.*

··· 달아요? *... is sweet?* 설탕이 달아요. *Sugar is sweet.*

··· 써요? *... is bitter?* 약이 써요. *Medicine is bitter.*

··· 맛있어요? *... tastes good?*

불고기가 맛있어요. *Bulgogi tastes good.*

Translation

The rice and side dishes fill up the dining table. Everyone sits around the dining table. "The food is very good." / "Could I have some more rice?" / "Yes, have a lot." / Everyone has a good meal.

Classwork and Homework

1. Reading Comprehension: Answer these questions about the story.

   1) 밥상에 무엇이 가득합니까?

   [   ] 과 [   ] 이 가득해요.

   2) 모두 어디에 둘러앉았습니까?

   모두 [   ] 에 둘러앉았어요.

   3) 음식이 얼마나 맛있습니까?

   [   ] 맛있어요.

   4) 모두 어떻게 식사합니까?

   [   ] 식사해요.

2. Translate these sentences into Korean.

   1) Can I have a little more rice?

   2) The food is delicious.

   3) It is hot.

   4) It is too spicy.

   5) What tastes good?

Let's Go Home. No More Shopping!

Going to buy toys is fun. Going to buy food can even be fun. But going with your mom and sister to buy girl clothes is definitely not fun. I can't think of anything more boring than watching my sister buy a new dress. Ugh!

30. 쇼핑 (Shopping)

누나는 엄마하고 쇼핑을 갔어요.

상점에는 예쁜 옷들이 많아요.

누나는 까만 구두와 빨간 치마를 골랐어요.

"모두 얼마예요?"

"47달러 50센트예요."

"여기 있어요."

"감사합니다. 또 오세요."

누나는 엄마에게 고맙다고 말했어요.

Can we go now???

New Vocabulary

…하고 with, and	쇼핑 shopping
예쁜(예쁘다) to be pretty	구두 dress shoes
치마 skirt	골랐어요(고르다) to select, to choose
얼마예요 how much?	여기 있어요 here is
또 오세요 please, come again	고맙다 thank

Grammar and Notes

Vocabulary

1. Names of Stores

꽃집 florist

시장 market

서점 bookstore

미용실 hair salon

옷 가게 clothes store

백화점 department store

문구점 stationery store

생선 가게 fish market

보석상 jewelry store

식당 / 음식점 restaurant

약국 drugstore, pharmacy

식료품점 grocery store

여행사 travel agency

스포츠용품점 sporting goods store

2. Expressions for the Store

더 싼 것으로 주세요.
Could you please give me a cheaper one?

더 좋은 것으로 주세요.
Could you please give me a better one?

이것은 얼마예요? *How much is this?*

저것 좀 보여 주세요. *Could you please show me that one?*

잘 어울려요. *It looks good on you.*

잘 맞아요. *It fits very well.*

이것을 사고 싶어요. *I want to buy this.*

Translation

My sister went shopping with mom.
There are many pretty clothes in the store.
My sister chose black shoes and a red skirt.
"How much is it all together?"
"It is $47.50."
"Here it is."
"Thank you. Come again."
My sister said thank you to mom.

Classwork and Homework

1. Reading Comprehension: Answer these questions about the story.

   1) 누나는 누구하고 쇼핑을 갔습니까?

      ☐☐ 하고 갔어요.

   2) 상점에는 무엇이 많아요?

      ☐☐ ☐ 들이 많아요.

   3) 누나는 무슨 치마를 골랐습니까?

      ☐☐ 치마를 골랐어요.

   4) 구두와 치마 값이 모두 얼마였습니까?

      ☐☐ 달러 ☐☐ 센트였어요.

   5) 누나는 엄마에게 뭐라고 말했습니까?

      ☐☐☐ 고 말했어요.

2. Ask and Answer the following questions with your friends.

   1) When you want to eat some food, where do you go ?

   2) When you want to buy a book, where do you go?

   3) When you need to buy clothes, where do you go?

Let's Go to the Zoo!

We're going... we're going... we're going to the zoo.
We're going... we're going... we're going to the zoo! Yay!
"Dorothy, come on! We're leaving right now." I have to go.
Come with me. Hurry!

31. 동물원 (Zoo)

오늘은 우리 가족이 동물원에 갔습니다.

동물원에는 사자, 호랑이, 원숭이, 코끼리, 곰,

그리고 다른 많은 동물들이 있었습니다.

우리 안에 있는 동물들을 가까이서

보았습니다.

점심때 어머니가 만든 김밥을 먹었습니다.

New Vocabulary

동물원 zoo	사자 lion	호랑이 tiger
원숭이 monkey	코끼리 elephant	곰 bear
다른 other	동물 animal	우리 cage
보았습니다(보다) to see, to look at, to watch		
만든(만들다) to make	김밥 *gimbap*	

Grammar and Notes

Present, Past and Future Participles

1) Introduction

있는(있다) and 만든(만들다) are verb forms, but they are used as <u>modifiers</u> in the text.

Ex. 1) <u>우리 안에 있는</u> 동물들 wild beasts <u>that are in a cage</u>
　　2) <u>어머니가 만든</u> 김밥 gimbap <u>that mom made</u>

These verb forms are called participles and are used basically as adjectives. However, just like verbs, participles have tenses: past, present and future.

2) Forming the Participles

Present (verb stem + 는)
Past (verb stem + ㄴ), and
Future (verb stem + ㄹ)

*Note: The participle forms in the parentheses are actually the imperfect participle form.

Dictionary Form	Present	Past*	Future
하다 *to do*	하는	한 (했던)	할
가다 *to go*	가는	간 (갔던)	갈
있다 *there is*	있는	있은 (있었던)	있을
준비하다 *to prepare*	준비하는	준비한 (준비했던)	준비할

Translation

Today, our family went to the zoo.
At the zoo, there were lions, tigers, monkeys, elephants, bears, and also many other animals.
We saw from up close wild beasts that were in a cage.
At lunchtime, we ate the *gimbap* that mom made.

1. Reading Comprehension: Answer these questions about the story.

   1) 코리네 가족은 어디에 갔습니까?

      ☐☐☐ 에 갔어요.

   2) 동물원에는 무슨 동물들이 있었습니까?

      ☐☐ , ☐☐☐ , ☐☐☐ , ☐ 등이 있어요.

   3) 점심때 무엇을 먹었습니까?

      ☐☐ 을 먹었어요.

   4) 김밥은 누가 만들었습니까?

      ☐☐☐ 가 만들었어요.

2. Fill in the blanks with the correct words.

   ☐☐☐   ☐☐☐

3. Change the sentences to a participial phrase.

   1) 어머니가 김밥을 만들었다. → 어머니가 ☐☐ 김밥

   2) 우리 안에 동물들이 있다. → 우리 안에 ☐☐ 동물

Let's Go to the Market!

I'm going to the market with my mom today. My mom says it's really crowded there. She told me not to go off so that I wouldn't get lost. But I want to go and explore the market like the famous explorers who travelled to far and distant lands. Come join me in my adventure. Off we go!

32. 시장 (Market)

시장은 사람들로 붐볐습니다.

물건을 고르는 사람, 값을 묻는 사람,

물건 값을 내는 사람, 포장을 하는 사람,

"어서 오십시오." "안녕히 가십시오."

인사하는 사람들로 붐볐습니다.

New Vocabulary

붐볐습니다(붐비다) to be crowded

고르는(고르다) to choose

값 price

묻는(묻다) to ask

내는(내다) to pay (money), to give

포장을 하는(포장을 하다) to wrap

Grammar

Adjective Clauses

An adjective clause is a clause that is used as an adjective to modify a noun or a pronoun. In English, an adjective clause is always introduced by a relative pronoun, such as *who, whose, which*, and *that.* In Korean, the participle form is used in the adjective clause.

In both cases, the underlined clause is the adjective clause.

1) 시장에는 사람들로 붐볐습니다. The market was crowded with people.
   사람들이 물건을 사고 팝니다. The people buy and sell things.

   The market was crowded with people (the people) buy and sell things.
   The market was crowded with people (who) buy and sell things.
   The market was crowded with people who buy and sell things.

   시장에는 사람들 (사람들이 물건을 사고 팝니다)로 붐볐습니다.
   시장에는 사람들 (who? 물건을 사고 파는 사람들)로 붐볐습니다.
   시장에는 **물건을 사고 파는** 사람들로 붐볐습니다.

2) 도서관에는 학생들이 많아요. *There are many students at the library.*
   학생들이 공부합니다. *The students study.*

   There are many students (the students study) at the library.
   There are many students (who study) at the library.
   There are many students who study at the library.

   도서관에는 학생들 (학생들이 공부합니다)이 많아요.
   도서관에는 학생들 (who? 공부하는 학생들)이 많아요.
   도서관에는 **공부하는 학생들이** 많아요.

Translation

The market was crowded with people.
It was crowded with people who were choosing things, asking about prices, paying for things, wrapping things and saying "Welcome" and "Goodbye."

Classwork and Homework

1. Reading Comprehension: Answer these questions about the story.

   1) 시장은 무엇으로 붐볐습니까?

   [|] 들로 붐볐습니다.

2. Match the words together to form a participial phrase.

   물건 값을 ○   ○ 하는 사람

   포장을 ○   ○ 고르는 사람

   물건을 ○   ○ 묻는 사람

3. Change the sentences to a participial phrase.

   Ex. 사람들이 인사합니다. → [인 | 사 | 하 | 는] 사람들

   1) 학생들이 공부합니다. → [| | |] 학생들

   2) 사람들이 일합니다. → [| |] 사람들

   3) 학생들이 운동을 합니다. → 운동을 [|] 학생들

Let's Look up in the Sky!

Hey, let's go outside to the backyard. I just got a new telescope yesterday. We can pretend that we are astronauts on a dangerous mission. We must explore strange galaxies and discover new stars and planets. We must fight off man-eating aliens to save the world. Help!

33. 해와 달과 별 (Sun, Moon & Star)

하늘은 맑고 푸릅니다.

맑고 푸른 하늘에 해가 빛납니다.

밤이 되면 수많은 별들이 반짝입니다.

둥근 달이 뜨면 밤도 낮처럼 밝습니다.

달빛으로 시골 마을은 그림처럼 아름답습니다.

New Vocabulary

맑고(맑다) to be clear	해 sun
빛납니다(빛나다) to shine	밤 night
되면(되다) to become	수많은 a great number of
반짝입니다(반짝이다) to twinkle, to sparkle	
둥근(둥글다) to be round	뜨면(뜨다) to rise
낮처럼 like day	밝습니다(밝다) to be bright
시골 마을 countryside, rural area	그림 picture, painting
…처럼 like	

Grammar and Notes

Phrase

1. ···면 (*if, when*)

1) 밤이 **되면**, 수많은 별이 반짝입니다.
   When it becomes night, a great number of stars twinkle.

2) 비가 **오면**, 소풍을 못 가요.
   If it rains, we cannot go on a picnic.

3) 공부를 열심히 **하면**, 성적이 올라가요.
   If you study hard, your grades will go up.

2. ···처럼 (*like* = 같이)

1) 시골 마을은 그림**처럼** (= **같이**) 아름답습니다.
   The countryside is beautiful like a painting.

2) 누나는 가수**처럼** (= **같이**) 노래해요.
   My older sister sings like a professional singer.

3) 철수는 어른**처럼** (= **같이**) 행동해요.
   Chulsoo acts like an adult.

Developing Sentences

(Basic Form)　　밤도 밝습니다.　*The night is also bright.*
(How bright?)　　밤도 **낮처럼** 밝습니다.
(When?)　　　　**달이 뜨면** 밤도 낮처럼 밝습니다
(What kind?)　　**둥근** 달이 뜨면 밤도 낮처럼 밝습니다.
(Final sent.)　　*When the round moon rises, the night is also bright like the day.*

Translation

The sky is clear and blue.
The sun shines in the clear and blue sky.
When it becomes night, a great number of stars twinkle.
When the round moon rises, night is also bright like day.
Under the moonlight, the countryside is beautiful like a painting.

Classwork and Homework

1. Reading Comprehension: Answer these questions about the story.

   1) 하늘에는 무엇이 빛납니까?

      ☐ 가 빛나요.

   2) 밤하늘에는 무엇이 반짝입니까?

      ☐☐ ☐ 이 반짝여요.

   3) 무엇이 뜨면 밤도 낮처럼 밝습니까?

      ☐☐ ☐ 이 뜨면 밝아요.

   4) 무엇 때문에 시골 마을이 아름답습니까?

      ☐☐ 때문에 아름다워요.

2. Match the phrases together to form a complete sentence.

   비가 오면 ○   ○ 수많은 별이 반짝입니다.

   공부를 열심히 하면 ○   ○ 소풍을 못 가요.

   밤이 되면 ○   ○ 성적이 올라가요.

3. Translate these sentences into Korean.

   1) You cry like a baby.   ☐

   2) My sister speaks like an adult. ☐

   3) Today is warm like spring.   ☐

Let's Answer the Telephone!

Ring. Ring. Hold on, the telephone's ringing. I have to go answer it. It may be a secret message from the government. I'm an international spy, you see. They call to give me my mission. I wonder what I have to do this time.

34. 전화 (Telephone)

따르릉 전화가 왔습니다.

"내가 받을게요."

누나는 방에서 나오면서 말했습니다.

"여보세요?"

"애야, 너희 엄마 좀 바꿔 줄래?"

"네. 잠깐만 기다리세요."

"엄마, 전화 받으세요! 엄마를 찾는 전화예요."

어머니께서 전화를 받으셨습니다.

Shoot! My sister and mom picked up the phone instead.
I guess I'll have to find out about my mission next time.

New Vocabulary

따르릉 ring	전화 telephone
받을게요(받다) to receive (a call), to pick up (a phone)	
바꿔 줄래(바꾸다) to change	잠깐만 just a moment
찾는(찾다) to find, to look for	

Grammar and Notes

Telephone Conversation

Directions: Read through the following dialogue and pay close attention to new expressions.

경희: (Kyunghee)	"여보세요? 순이네 집이지요?" *"Hello? Is this Sooni's residence?"*
순이 오빠: (Sooni's bro.)	"네, 그렇습니다." *"Yes, it is."*
경희:	"저 순이 친구 경희인데요." *"This is Sooni's friend, Kyunghee.* 순이 좀 바꿔 주세요." *Can I speak to Sooni?"*
순이 오빠:	"잠깐만 기다리세요." *"Hold on for a moment."*
경희:	"고맙습니다." *"Thank you."*
순이 오빠:	"지금 순이가 없는데요." *"Sooni is not here right now."*
경희:	"언제쯤 돌아오나요?" *"Approximately when will she come back?"*
순이 오빠:	"5시쯤에요." *"At about 5 o'clock."*
경희:	"그럼 다시 전화할게요. 안녕히 계세요." *"Then I will call back. Goodbye."*
순이 오빠:	"네, 안녕히 계세요." *"Okay, goodbye."*

Ring. The telephone rings. "I will pick it up," said my sister as she came out of the room. "Hello?" / "Hey, can I speak to your mom?" / "Could you hold on for just a moment? / Mom! Pick up the phone. It's a phone call for you." Mom picked up the phone.

Classwork and Homework

1. Reading Comprehension: Answer these questions about the story.

   1) 따르릉 소리를 내며 무엇이 왔습니까?

   ☐☐ 가 왔어요.

   2) 누가 전화를 받았습니까?

   ☐☐ 가 전화를 받았어요.

   3) 누나가 무슨 말을 처음 했습니까?

   ☐☐☐ 라고 말했어요.

   4) 누구를 찾는 전화였습니까?

   ☐☐ 를 찾는 전화였어요.

2. Put the following telephone dialogue in order.

   언제쯤 돌아오나요?   ☐

   안녕히 계세요.   ☐

   여보세요?   ☐

   순이 좀 바꿔 주세요.   ☐

Let's Learn about the Different Days!

What day is it? Hurry, someone find a calendar. What day is it? Friday? Really? Yay! I love Fridays. It's the weekend. Let the fun begin. Woo-hoo! Wait, what? I have to go somewhere and learn something tomorrow morning? So I can't watch the Saturday morning cartoons? Can't we change the time of the class? Can't we do something? But my brain doesn't work on Saturday mornings. Oh, phooey. I don't like Fridays very much.

35. 요일 (Day)

일주일은 7일입니다.

월요일, 화요일, 수요일, 목요일, 금요일,

토요일, 일요일이 있습니다.

대부분의 사람들이 월요일부터 금요일까지

일합니다.

많은 사람들이 주말에는 쉽니다.

우리는 토요일에 한국 학교에서 한국어를

공부합니다.

New Vocabulary

주일 week	…부터 …까지 … from … until
주말 weekend	쉽니다(쉬다) to rest
한국 학교 Korean School	

Grammar and Notes

Vocabulary

Days of the Week

월요일 Monday	목요일 Thursday	일요일 Sunday
화요일 Tuesday	금요일 Friday	
수요일 Wednesday	토요일 Saturday	

Phrase

1. ···부터 ···까지 (*... from ... until* : referring to time)

1) 월요일**부터** 금요일**까지** 열심히 일합니다.
   We work hard from Monday until Friday.

2) 어제**부터** 지금**까지** 비가 와요.
   It has been raining from yesterday until now.

3) 목요일**부터** 다음 월요일**까지** 봄방학입니다.
   Spring vacation is from Thursday until next Monday.

2. ···부터

Note: When 부터 is used alone, the meaning may vary slightly depending upon the context.

1) 내일**부터** 피아노 레슨을 시작해요.
   I will begin my piano lessons starting tomorrow.

2) 어제 오후**부터** 날씨가 맑아졌어요.
   The weather has been clear since yesterday afternoon.

3. ···부터 ···까지 (*... from ... to* : referring to distance)

1) 여기서**부터** 저기**까지** 경주하자.
   Let's race from here to there.

2) 여기서**부터** 학교**까지** 좀 데려다 주세요.
   Could you take me from here to school?

Translation

One week has seven days : Monday, Tuesday, Wednesday, Thursday, Friday, Saturday, and Sunday. Most people work from Monday until Friday. Many people rest on the weekend. We study Korean at Korean School on Saturdays.

Classwork and Homework

1. Reading Comprehension: Answer these questions about the story.

   1) 일주일에는 몇 일이 있습니까?

      ☐ 일이 있어요.

   2) 대부분의 사람들이 언제부터 언제까지 일합니까?

      ☐☐☐ 부터 ☐☐☐ 까지 일해요.

   3) 사람들이 언제 쉽니까?

      ☐☐ 에 쉽니다.

   4) 한국 학교에서는 언제 한국어를 공부합니까?

      ☐☐☐ 에 공부합니다.

2. Fill in the blanks with the correct name of the day.

   1) Monday ☐☐☐ 2) Wednesday ☐☐☐

   3) Friday ☐☐☐ 4) Sunday ☐☐☐

3. Complete the sentences using a proper phrase.

   1) 여기서 ☐☐ 학교 ☐☐ 얼마나 멀어요?

      How far is it from here to school?

   2) 나는 아침 ☐☐ 저녁 ☐☐ 일했어요.

      I worked from morning till evening.

Let's Celebrate My Grandpa's Birthday!

Today is June 18. We are all celebrating my grandpa's birthday. My grandpa is a lucky person. Think about all the presents he's gotten over the years. He must have gotten a million presents by now! I sure do want to grow up to be like my grandpa.

36. 생일 (Birthday)

오늘은 할아버지의 생신입니다.

어머니와 고모는 부엌에서 음식을

만들었습니다.

친척들이 다 모였습니다.

우리는 할아버지께 선물을 드렸습니다.

할아버지께서 건강하게 오래 사시기를

빌었습니다.

New Vocabulary

생신, 생일 birthday	고모 aunt (on father's side)
친척 relative	선물 present
건강하게(건강하다) to be healthy	오래 a long time
사시기를(살다) to live	
빌었습니다(빌다) to wish, to beg	

Grammar and Notes

Grammar

Honorific Speech [Part 1]

In Korean, there are various levels of formality which are used in speech and in writing. 반말, meaning plain speech, refers to familiar speech used by family members or friends. However, most of the texts in this book is written using 존댓말. 존댓말, or honorific speech, is used to indicate a level of formality or respect.

1) How to Form Honorific Speech

   a) Changing the Subject Particle: Instead of using the subject particles 은, 는, 이, or 가, always use the particle 께서.

	Honorific Speech
아버지가	아버지<u>께서</u>
어머니가	어머니<u>께서</u>
아저씨가	아저씨<u>께서</u>
할아버지가	할아버지<u>께서</u>

Note: For further explanation of honorific speech forms and expressions, see ex. 40.

   b) Changing the Verb Form: Add 시 to the end of the verb stem.

	Honorific Speech
아버지가 온다.	아버지께서 오<u>신</u>다. Father is coming.
어머니가 일한다.	어머니께서 일하<u>신</u>다. Mother is working.
할아버지가 간다.	할아버지께서 가<u>신</u>다. Grandpa is going.
할머니가 만든다.	할머니께서 만드<u>신</u>다. Grandma is making.

Translation

Today, it is my grandfather's birthday. My mom and aunt prepared food in the kitchen. All the relatives gathered. We gave grandfather a gift. We wished grandfather good health and a long life.

Classwork and Homework

1. Reading Comprehension: Answer these questions about the story.

   1) 오늘은 누구의 생신입니까?

      ☐☐☐☐ 의 생신입니다.

   2) 누가 부엌에서 음식을 만듭니까?

      ☐☐☐ 와 ☐☐

   3) 할아버지의 생신에 누가 모였습니까?

      ☐☐ 들이 다 모였습니다.

   4) 할아버지께 무엇을 드렸습니까?

      ☐☐ 을 드렸습니다.

2. Change the following words and sentences to the honorific form.

   1) 할아버지가 ⟶ 할아버지☐☐

   2) 할머니가 ⟶ 할머니☐☐

   3) 아버지가 ⟶ 아버지☐☐

   4) 할아버지가 온다. ⟶ 할아버지☐☐ ☐☐☐.

   5) 할머니가 간다. ⟶ 할머니☐☐ ☐☐☐.

   6) 아버지가 일한다. ⟶ 아버지☐☐ ☐☐☐☐.

Let's Learn about Soldiers!

Do you know what you want to be when you grow up? I know what I want to be. I want to be in the military. I'm going to be the best Air Force pilot when I grow up. I'm going to fly in a jet and shoot down enemy airplanes. Captain Kory going at the speed of light to protect the country!

37. 군인 (Soldier)

군인들은 나라를 지킵니다.

낮에도 밤에도, 비가 와도 눈이 와도 쉬지
않습니다.

육군은 육지에서, 해군은 바다에서,

공군은 하늘에서 나라를 지킵니다.

그래서 적군은 쳐들어오지 못합니다.

군인들은 우리가 편안하게 살도록 나라를
지킵니다.

New Vocabulary

군인 soldier	지킵니다 (지키다) to guard
와도 (오다) to come	쉬지 않습니다 (쉬지 않다) not to rest
육군 Army	육지 land
해군 Navy	공군 Air force
적군 enemy troops	쳐들어오다 to invade
편안하게 peacefully	살도록 (살다) to live

Grammar and Notes

Phrase

1. ···도 (*even though*)

1) 바람이 **불어도** 테니스를 칩니다.
   Even though the wind blows, we play tennis.

2) **피곤해도**, 숙제를 마치겠습니다.
   Even though I am tired, I will complete my homework.

2. ···도록 (*so that ... may*)

1) 우리가 평안하게 **살도록** 나라를 지킵니다.
   They guard the country so that we may live comfortably.

2) 아기가 잠을 **자도록** 조용히 합시다.
   Let's be quiet so that the baby may sleep.

Grammar

Negative Form [Part 2]

1) ···지 못합니다. *cannot*
   나는 수영을 **하지 못합니다**. *I cannot swim.*
   저 새는 **날지 못해요**. *That bird cannot fly.*

2) ···지 않습니다. *not*
   우리는 **싸우지 않습니다**. *We do not fight.*
   우리는 거짓말을 **하지 않습니다**. *We do not lie.*

3) ··· 안 합니다. *not*
   나는 공부를 합니다. → 나는 공부를 **안 합니다**. *I do not study.*
   우리는 학교에 갑니다. → 우리는 학교에 **안 갑니다**.
   　　　　　　　　　　　　　We do not go to school.

Translation

Soldiers guard the country. Whether it is day or night, it rains or snows, they do not rest. The Army guards the country on land, the Navy at sea, and the Air Force in the sky. That is why enemy troops cannot invade. Soldiers guard the country so that we may live in peace.

Classwork and Homework

1. Reading Comprehension: Answer these questions about the story.

   1) 군인들이 무엇을 지킵니까?

      [　][　] 를 지켜요.

   2) 육군은 어디에서 나라를 지킵니까?

      [　][　] 에서 나라를 지켜요.

   3) 해군은 어디에서 나라를 지킵니까?

      [　][　] 에서 나라를 지킵니다.

   4) 군인들은 왜 나라를 지킵니까?

      우리가 [　][　] 하게 살도록 나라를 지킵니다.

2. Change these sentences into the negative form.

   1) 나는 스키를 탑니다. 나는 스키를 [　][　] 못합니다. (cannot)

   2) 누나는 피아노를 칩니다. 누나는 피아노를 [　][　] 못합니다. (cannot)

   3) 우리는 싸움을 합니다. 우리는 싸움을 하지 [　][　][　][　] . (not)

   4) 나는 거짓말을 합니다. 나는 거짓말을 하지 [　][　][　][　] . (not)

   5) 소리가 납니다. 소리가 [　][　][　][　] . (not)

Let's Take a Trip to the Beach!

It's summer time, and it is hot. So my family is going on a trip to the beach! Grab your swimsuit and body board. Come with us! We can ride the waves on our boards. And then we can build the best and the biggest sand castle ever created! Or you can bury me in sand if you want. So many things to do. Let's go to the beach!

38. 바닷가 (Beach)

바다는 참 넓고 푸릅니다.

파도가 해변에서 하얗게 부서지고 있습니다.

모래밭에는 검게 탄 사람들이 많이 있습니다.

아이들이 물에서 놀고 있습니다.

어떤 아이들은 모래성을 만들고 있습니다.

여름철 바닷가는 활기찹니다.

New Vocabulary

바다 ocean, sea	넓고(넓다) to be wide, to be vast
파도 wave	해변 seashore
부서지고(부서지다) to crash down	
모래밭 sand	탄(타다) to burn, to be tanned
모래성 sand castle	여름철 summertime
활기찹니다(활기차다) to be active	

Grammar and Notes

Grammar

Progressive Form

In English, the progressive form is given by the form: "am, is, are" + verb + "-ing", eg. am swimming.

In Korean, there are two different forms of the progressive.
1) Verb stem + 고 있습니다 / 있어요 / 있다.
2) Verb stem + 는 중입니다 / 중이어요 / 중이다.

Examples of Usage:

Note: To emphasize progress clearly, use 지금.

1) 아이들이 물에서 <u>놀고 있습니다</u>.
   The kids are playing in the water.
2) 어떤 아이들은 모래성을 <u>만들고 있습니다</u>.
   Some other kids are making a sand castle.
3) 누나는 노래를 <u>부르고 있습니다</u>. *My sister is singing a song.*
4) 나는 지금* 공부를 <u>하는 중입니다</u>. *I am studying now.*

Developing Sentences

(Basic Form)   파도가 부서지고 있습니다.
               The wave is crashing down.
(Where?)   파도가 <u>해변에서</u> 부서지고 있습니다.
(How?)   파도가 해변에서 <u>하얗게</u> 부서지고 있습니다.
(Final sent.) *The wave is crashing down white on the seashore.*

Translation

The sea is very vast and blue. The wave is crashing down white on the seashore. On the sand, there are many tanned people. The children are playing in the water. Some other kids are building sand castles. The beach is alive in the summertime.

Classwork and Homework

1. Reading Comprehension: Answer these questions about the story.

   1) 바다는 얼마나 넓습니까?

      ☐ 넓어요.

   2) 파도는 해변에서 어떻게 부서집니까?

      ☐☐☐ 부서집니다.

   3) 모래밭에는 어떤 사람들이 많습니까?

      ☐☐ 탄 사람들이 많아요.

   4) 아이들이 무엇을 만들고 있습니까?

      ☐☐☐ 을 만들고 있어요.

2. Look at the pictures. What are they doing?

   1) ☐☐ 을 하고 있습니다.   2) ☐☐ 를 하고 있습니다.

   3) ☐☐ 를 하고 있습니다.   4) ☐☐ 를 하고 있습니다.

Let's Not Think about School!

There's a whole month before school starts again. I'm going to play really hard the entire month and not even think about school. But my sister has already started to plan out the next school year. She decided she's going to try even harder when school starts again. Can you believe that? Check out her resolution.

39. 결심 (Resolution)

곧 새 학년이 됩니다.

나는 새로운 결심을 합니다.

나는 지난해보다 더 열심히 공부할 것입니다.

부모님 말씀도 더 잘 들을 것입니다.

날마다 일기도 쓸 것입니다.

친구들과도 사이 좋게 지낼 것입니다.

I can't believe I'm related to her. Look at me.
I have nothing written down.

New Vocabulary

곧 soon	새 학년 new school year
됩니다(되다) to become	새로운 new
지난해 last year	말씀 words, saying, talks
들을 것입니다(듣다) to listen	날마다 daily
일기 journal	쓸 것입니다(쓰다) to write
친구들과도 with friends	
지낼 것입니다(지내다) to get along	

Grammar and Notes

Grammar

Future Tense Verb Forms

1) How to Make Future Tense Forms. General Rule.

Verb Stem + ㄹ + Ending (것이다, 것입니다, or 거예요)

Note: When the verb stem ends in a final consonant other than ㄹ, add −ㄹ/을 것이다 to make the future form.

2) Chart of Basic Verbs in Future Tense

Dict. Form	Plain (−ㄹ 것이다)	Mod./Formal (−ㄹ 것입니다)	Casual (−ㄹ 거예요)
하다 *to do*	할 것이다	할 것입니다	할 거예요
되다 *to become*	될 것이다	될 것입니다	될 거예요
놀다 *to play*	놀 것이다	놀 것입니다	놀 거예요
먹다* *to eat*	먹을 것이다	먹을 것입니다	먹을 거예요

Ex. 1) 나는 장차 교수가 **될 거예요**.

I will become a professor in the future.

2) 나는 책을 많이 **읽을 것입니다**.

I am going to read many books.

3) 버스가 10시에 **도착할 것입니다**.

The bus will arrive at 10 o'clock.

Developing Sentences

(Basic Form)　　　　나는 공부할 것입니다. *I will study.*
(How much?)　　　　나는 **더 열심히** 공부할 것입니다.
(How much more?)　나는 **지난해보다 더** 열심히 공부할 것입니다.
(Final Form)　　　　*I will study harder than last year.*

Translation

It will be a new school year soon. I make a new resolution. I will study harder than I did last year. I will also listen better to my parents' advice. I will also write in my journal daily. I will get along well with my friends.

1. Reading Comprehension: Answer these questions about the story.

   1) 코리는 어떤 결심을 합니까?

   [ ][ ][ ] 결심을 해요.

   2) 코리는 지난해보다 무엇을 더 열심히 하려고 합니까?

   [ ][ ] 를 열심히 하려고 해요.

   3) 코리는 누구의 말씀을 잘 들으려고 합니까?

   [ ][ ][ ] 말씀을 잘 들으려고 해요.

   4) 날마다 무엇을 쓰려고 합니까?

   [ ][ ] 를 쓰려고 해요.

   5) 누구와 사이 좋게 지내려고 합니까?

   [ ][ ][ ] 과 사이 좋게 지내려고 해요.

2. Change the sentences into the future tense form.

   1) 나는 교수가 된다.　→

   2) 나는 부자가 된다.　→

   3) 나는 일기를 쓴다.　→

   4) 비가 온다.　→

Let's Relax at My Home!

Home sweet home! There's no place like it. I know I don't always show appreciation for my family, but there's nothing like a loving family. Dad works hard every day at work. He doesn't even get a summer vacation. Mom works hard at home every day too. She doesn't even get a break on the weekends! What a wonderful family. . . Dad, mom, and me. . . . Oh, ok. My older sister counts too, even though she's only nice to me sometimes. What a wonderful family. . . Dad, Mom, Dorothy, and me!

40. 가정 (Home)

아버지께서는 회사에 다니십니다.

우리는 학교에 갑니다.

어머니께서는 집에서 일을 하십니다.

저녁이 되면 식구들이 모두 집에 돌아옵니다.

저녁식사를 한 후 그날 있었던 일들을 서로

이야기하면서 즐거운 시간을 보냅니다.

New Vocabulary

회사 company	다니십니다(다니다) to go to
일 work	저녁 evening
식구 family	돌아옵니다(돌아오다) to come back
이야기하면서(이야기하다) to talk	
시간 time	보냅니다(보내다) to pass, to spend

Grammar and Notes

Grammar

Honorific Speech [Part 2]

A way to demonstrate a level of respect for the other person is to lower oneself in speech. When using Honorific Speech (존댓말), the form of the pronoun "I" changes.

나는 → 저는 **and** 내가 → 제가

Ex. 1) 나는 김철수입니다. → **저는** 김철수입니다.
   2) 내가 하겠습니다. → **제가** 하겠습니다.

Another particle used in honorific speech …**님**.

아버지 → 아버**님**; 어머니 → 어머**님**; 선생 → 선생**님**

* Honorific Expressions

말 → **말씀**	words	준다 → **드린다**	to give
밥 → **진지**	meal	잔다 → **주무신다**	to sleep
있다 → **계신다**	is	먹는다 → **드신다(잡수신다)**	to eat

Ex. 1) 할머니께서 **주무십니다**. *Grandmother is sleeping.*
   2) 아버지께서 집에 **계십니다**. *Father is at home.*

Developing Sentences

(Basic Form) (우리는) 즐거운 시간을 보냅니다.
We have a good time.

(Doing what?) (우리는) **서로 이야기하면서** 즐거운 시간을 가집니다.

(Sharing what?) **그날 있었던 일을** 서로 이야기하면서 즐거운 시간을 보냅니다.

(When?) **저녁 식사를 한 후**, 그 날 있었던 일을 서로 이야기하면서 즐거운 시간을 보냅니다.

(Final sent.) *After dinner, we have a good time talking about that day's events with each other.*

Translation

Dad goes to work. We go to school. Mom works at home. When it becomes evening, the entire family returns home. After dinner, we have a good time talking about that day's events with each other.

1. Reading Comprehension: Answer these questions about the story.

   1) 아버지는 어디에 가십니까?

     ☐☐ 에 가세요.

   2) 코리와 누나는 어디에 갑니까?

     ☐☐ 에 가요.

   3) 어머니는 어디에서 일하십니까?

     ☐ 에서 일하세요.

   4) 식구들이 언제 집으로 돌아옵니까?

     ☐☐ 이 되면 집으로 돌아와요.

2. Change the following words and sentences to the honorific form.

   1) 아버지 ☐☐☐☐☐   2) 교수 ☐☐☐☐☐

   3) 어머니 ☐☐☐☐☐   4) 박사 ☐☐☐☐☐

   5) 선생 ☐☐☐☐☐   6) 감독 ☐☐☐☐☐

   7) 할아버지가 있다. ⟶ ☐☐☐☐☐☐☐

   8) 할머니가 잔다. ⟶ ☐☐☐☐☐☐☐

   9) 아버지가 온다. ⟶ ☐☐☐☐☐☐☐

Let's Welcome the Guests!

Alert! Intruders in the home! Alert! Some guests are coming over to stay at our house tonight. My dad says they are his friends. But I'm going to check up on them just to make sure. Dad says two kids my age are coming too. They better not try to play with any of my toys. I'm going to keep an eye on them, for I am Captain Kory, protector of the home!

41. 손님 (Guest)

아빠의 친구 가족이 우리집을 방문했습니다.

엄마가 손님들에게 집을 안내했습니다.

"여기 계시는 동안 이 방을 사용하세요."

"네, 감사합니다."

"내일은 함께 시내 구경을 갑시다."

어른들은 밤 늦게까지 말씀을 나누셨습니다.

New Vocabulary

방문했습니다(방문하다) to visit

안내했습니다(안내하다) to introduce

사용하세요(사용하다) to use   시내 downtown

구경 sightseeing   밤 늦게 late at night

말씀을 나누셨습니다(이야기를 나누다) to talk

Grammar and Notes

Indirect Object

Subject	Indirect Object	Object	Verb
엄마가	손님들에게	집을	안내했습니다.

My mother gave a tour of the house to our guests.

The indirect object particle is 에게. The honorific form of the particle is 께.

1) 어머니는 우리에게 새 옷을 사 주셨습니다.
   Mom bought us new clothes.
2) 우리는 할아버지께 선물을 드렸습니다.
   We gave grandfather a present.

Phrase

1. 여기에 (*here*), 저기에 (*over there*)

1) 가방이 **여기에** 있습니다. *The bag is here.*
2) 식당은 **저기에** 있어요. *The dining room is over there.*

2. …동안 (*while*)

1) 엄마가 음식을 만드는 **동안**, 나는 청소를 합니다.
   While mom makes the food, I clean.
2) 우리가 공부하는 **동안**, 아기는 잠을 잤어요.
   While we were studying, the baby slept.

3. …까지 (*until, by*)

1) 밤 늦게**까지** 우리는 컴퓨터 게임을 했어요.
   We played computer games until late at night.
2) 오후 2시**까지** 꼭 오세요. *Definitely come by 2 p.m.*

Translation

The family of my dad's friend visited our home. Mom gave a tour of the house to our guests. "While you are staying here, you may use this room." / "Thank you." / "Tomorrow, let's go downtown for sightseeing together." / The adults talked until late at night.

Classwork and Homework

1. Reading Comprehension: Answer these questions about the story.

   1) 누가 코리네 집을 방문했습니까?

   아빠의 ⬜⬜ 가족이 방문했어요.

   2) 누가 손님들에게 집을 안내했습니까?

   ⬜⬜ 가 하셨어요.

   3) 내일은 모두 어디로 가기로 했습니까?

   ⬜⬜⬜ ⬜⬜ 을 가기로 했어요.

   4) 누가 밤 늦게까지 이야기를 했습니까?

   ⬜⬜⬜ 이 하셨습니다.

2. Fill in the blanks with a correct object particle (을, 를, 에게).

   1) 나는 숙제 ⬜ 했어요.

   2) 아빠는 나 ⬜⬜ 장난감 ⬜ 사 주셨어요.

   3) 우리는 누니 ⬜⬜ 선물 ⬜ 시 주었어요.

3. Match the words together to make a complete sentence.

   12시까지 ◦   ◦ 오세요.

   공부하는 동안 ◦   ◦ 갈게요.

   점심때까지 ◦   ◦ 조용히 하세요.

Let's Learn about the Weather!

Why don't things ever go my way? Does it have to rain whenever I don't have an umbrella? Sheesh. And how can it rain all of a sudden when it was sunny all day? It's like Mother Nature can't make up her mind! Sunny or rainy? Just pick one. Either one is fine. But not both.

42. 날씨 (Weather)

바람이 불지 않고, 날씨가 무척 덥습니다.

갑자기 서쪽에서 비구름이 몰려옵니다.

금세 하늘이 어두워지면서 소나기가

쏟아집니다.

바람도 불고 무덥던 날씨가 갑자기

시원합니다.

여름 날씨는 참 변덕스럽습니다.

New Vocabulary

무척 very	덥습니다(덥다) to be hot
갑자기 suddenly	서쪽 west
비구름 rain cloud	몰려옵니다(몰려오다) to come in groups
금세 in a moment	어두워지면서(어두워지다) to become dark
소나기 rainshower	쏟아집니다(쏟아지다) to pour
무덥던(무덥다) to be very hot, sweltering	
시원합니다(시원하다) to be cool	
변덕스럽습니다(변덕스럽다) to be fickle, to be capricious	

Grammar and Notes

Vocabulary

1. Different Forms of Adverbs

빨리 *quickly*   기차는 참 **빨리** 달린다.
Indeed, trains travel quickly.

꼭 *surely*   나는 약속을 **꼭** 지킨다.
I surely keep my promises.

참 *indeed*   그는 **참** 좋은 친구이다.
He is indeed a good friend.

아직 *yet*   **아직** 나는 그 소식을 못 들었어요.
I have not heard that news yet.

정말로 *truly*   나는 **정말로** 기쁘다.
I am truly happy.

너무 *too (much)*   음식이 **너무** 많아요.
There is too much food.

2. Expressions about the Weather

따뜻해요.	*It is warm.*	어두워요.	*It is dark.*
추워요.	*It is cold.*	날이 밝아요.	*It's a bright day.*
시원해요.	*It is cool.*	눈이 와요.	*It is snowing.*
더워요.	*It is hot.*	안개가 끼었어요.	*It is foggy.*
바람이 불어요.	*It is windy.*	이슬비가 와요.	*It is drizzling.*
비가 와요.	*It is raining.*	소나기가 와요.	*It showers.*
태풍이 불어요.	*A typhoon is blowing.*		
천둥이 쳐요.	*The thunder sounds.*		

Translation

The wind is not blowing, and the weather is very hot. Suddenly, rain clouds come in groups from the West. In a moment, as the sky becomes dark, it pours. The wind blows, and the once steamy hot weather suddenly becomes cool. Summer weather is very fickle.

178

Classwork and Homework

1. Reading Comprehension: Answer these questions about the story.

   1) 비가 오기 전에 날씨가 어떠했습니까?

   ☐☐ 더웠습니다.

   2) 비구름이 어느 쪽에서 몰려왔습니까?

   ☐☐ 에서 몰려왔습니다.

   3) 비구름이 몰려오니 하늘이 어떻게 변했습니까?

   하늘이 ☐☐☐ 졌습니다.

   4) 소나기가 오니까 날씨가 어떻게 변했습니까?

   갑자기 ☐☐ 해졌습니다.

   5) 이런 여름 날씨를 뭐라고 합니까?

   ☐☐ 스럽다고 합니다.

2. Fill in the banks by choosing the right adverb from the word bank.

   1) 거북이는 ☐☐ 느리다. 　너무

   2) 아빠가 ☐☐ 안 오셨어요. 　꼭

   3) 12시까지 ☐ 오세요. 　빨리

   4) 늦지 않도록 ☐☐ 가세요. 　아직

Let's Celebrate Chuseok!

It's a holiday today. Don't get too excited though. We still have to go to school. What's the point of a holiday if you have to go to school? I don't understand that. Someone should change the school schedule. My mom said that it's Chuseok, a Korean holiday. She said that on this day, we're supposed to remember our ancestors. Hmm...I wonder what my ancestors were like. Hmm....

43. 명절 (Holiday)

추석은 옛날부터 내려오는 명절입니다.

이날 새 곡식으로 음식을 만들어 먹고

조상을 기억합니다.

멀리서 사는 가족들도 옵니다.

온 가족이 모이면 즐겁습니다.

추석은 모두가 기다리는 명절입니다.

New Vocabulary

추석 Chuseok (holiday)	옛날 a long time ago
내려오는(내려오다) to be transmitted	
명절 holiday	곡식 crops
조상 ancestor	기억합니다(기억하다) to remember
모두 everybody	기다리는(기다리다) to wait

Grammar and Notes

Phrase

…로/으로 *(by, with)*

Case 1: If the word does not have a final consonant, then add 로.
  1) 우리는 비행기로 한국에 가요. *We go to Korea by plane.*
  2) 누나는 비누로 얼굴을 씻어요.
     My older sister washes her face with soap.

Case 2: If the word has a final consonant, add …으로.
  1) 나는 손으로 공을 쳐요. *I hit the ball with my hand.*
  2) 엄마는 생선으로 스시를 만들어요.
     Mom makes Sushi with fish.

Exception: If the final consonant is a ㄹ, add …로.
  1) 나는 연필로 편지를 써요. *I write letters with a pencil.*
  2) 아버지는 차를 물로 씻어요.
     Dad washes the car with water.

Culture

추석 (Chuseok): Korean Traditional Holidays

Chuseok falls on the fifteenth day of the eighth month in the lunar year. Chuseok, known as the Harvest Moon Festival, may be best understood as the Korean equivalent of Thanksgiving. Most importantly, Chuseok is a time to give thanks for the autumn harvest and to celebrate with family. On this holiday, people visit the graves of their ancestors as a symbol of respect. 송편 *(songpyeon)*, a crescent-shaped rice cake stuffed with beans and flavored with pine needles, is a typical food prepared for Chuseok.

Translation

Chuseok is a holiday that has been observed since a long time ago. On this day, we make and eat food from the newly harvested crops, and we remember our ancestors. The relatives who live far away come together too. When my entire family gathers, we have a good time. Chuseok is a holiday for which everybody waits.

Classwork and Homework

1. Reading Comprehension: Answer these questions about the story.

   1) 추석은 언제부터 내려오는 명절입니까?

      [　|　] 부터 내려오는 명절이에요.

   2) 이날은 무엇으로 음식을 만들어 먹습니까?

      [　|　|　] 으로 음식을 만들어 먹어요.

   3) 추석에 모인 가족들은 누구를 기억합니까?

      [　|　] 을 기억해요.

   4) 이날은 가족들이 어디서도 옵니까?

      [　|　] 서도 와요.

   5) 누가 추석을 기다립니까?

      [　|　] 가 기다립니다.

2. Fill in the blanks with the correct preposition (로, 으로).

   1) 아빠는 비행기 [　] 한국에 가요.

   2) 엄마는 펜 [　|　] 편지를 써요.

   3) 나는 수건 [　|　] 차를 닦아요.

   4) 할머니는 배추 [　] 김치를 만들어요.

Let's Not Wake up So Early!

My mom wants me to start waking up earlier for school. She says I wake up too late and rush in the morning. She wants me to follow my sister's example and wake up at 6:30 every morning! 6:30!@#?!? I don't think the roosters are even awake at 6:30. My mom also wants me to do my homework right after I get home from school, before I watch TV. A whole day of using my brain at school and then more of it right when I get home! Can't I take a break? Look at my sister's schedule that I'm supposed to follow. Yuck!

44. 시간 (Time)

아침 6시 30분에 일어나서 학교 갈 준비를
합니다. 7시쯤 아침 식사를 하고, 버스로
학교에 갑니다. 8시 15분에 수업이 시작됩니다.
오후 12시 30분에 식당에서 점심을 먹습니다.
학교는 2시 30분에 끝납니다. 집에 오면
숙제를 먼저 하고, 텔레비전을 잠시 봅니다.
저녁을 먹고 책을 읽고 밤 10시경에 잠자리에
듭니다.

New Vocabulary

일어나서(일어나다) to get up   쯤 about

오후 afternoon   끝납니다(끝나다) to finish, to end

숙제 homework   잠시 for a little while

경 about, approximately

잠자리에 듭니다 (잠자리에 들다) to go to bed

Grammar and Notes

Phrase

...나서 (*after*)

1) 아침에 일어**나서**, 운동을 합니다.
   After I wake up in the morning, I exercise.
2) 운동을 하고 **나서**, 샤워를 합니다.
   After I exercise, I have a shower.
3) 밥을 먹고 **나서**, 산보를 갑니다.
   After I eat, I take a walk.

Vocabulary

Reading Time

Essential Vocabulary

오전 *A.M.*	오후 *P.M.*	분 *minute*
몇 시입니까?	*What time is it?*	시 *o'clock*

6시 30분입니다.   8시 15분입니다.   3시 30분입니다.   10시입니다.

Developing Sentences

(Basic Form)	(나는) 준비를 합니다. *I prepare.*
(What?)	(나는) **학교 갈** 준비를 합니다.
(When?)	(나는) **일어나서** 학교 갈 준비를 합니다.
(At what time?)	(나는) **아침 6시 30분에** 일어나서 학교 갈 준비를 합니다.
(Final Form)	*After waking up at 6:30, I prepare to go to school.*

Translation

At 6:30 in the morning, I get up and prepare to go to school. At about 7 o'clock I have breakfast and go to school by bus. At 8:15 class starts. At 12:30 in the afternoon, I eat lunch in the cafeteria. School ends at 2:30. When I come home, I do my homework first and then watch television for a little while. After I eat dinner, I read a book and at about 10:00 I go to bed.

Classwork and Homework

1. Reading Comprehension: Answer these questions about the story.

1) 코리는 몇 시에 일어납니까?

아침 ⬚ 시 ⬚ 분에 일어나요.

2) 학교에는 어떻게 갑니까?

⬚ 로 가요.

3) 8시 15분에 뭐가 시작됩니까?

⬚ 이 시작되요.

4) 점심은 어디에서 먹습니까?

⬚ 에서 먹어요.

5) 학교는 몇 시에 끝납니까?

⬚ 시 ⬚ 분에 끝나요.

6) 집에 오면 무엇을 먼저 합니까?

⬚ 를 먼저 해요.

7) 잠들기 전에 무엇을 합니까?

⬚ 을 읽어요.

2. Ask these questions to your classmates.

1) 몇 시에 일어납니까? *What time do you get up?*
2) 몇 시에 학교에 갑니까? *What time do you go to school?*
3) 몇 시에 잡니까? *What time do you go to bed?*

Let's Learn about Firefighters!

Today, a firefighter came to school to talk about his job. It was so cool! He showed us a real fire truck. He also showed us how to use the ladder that they use to reach tall buildings. Guess what? I even got to put on a firefighter's hat and jacket. It was so cool! But he also taught us that being a firefighter was dangerous but important. I definitely look up to firefighters.

45. 소방관 (Firefighter)

불이 나면 소방관들이 소방차를 타고
달려갑니다. 소방차가 지나가면 모든 차들이
비켜줍니다. 불이 난 곳에 가자마자 물을 뿌려서
불을 끕니다. 불에서 미처 나오지 못한 사람이
있으면 위험을 무릅쓰고 구해줍니다.
나는 소방관 아저씨들을 존경합니다.

New Vocabulary

불이 나면(불나다) a fire breaks out

소방관 firefighter   소방차 fire truck

물을 뿌려서(물을 뿌리다) to spray water

끕니다 (끄다) to extinguish, to turn off   미처 yet

위험을 무릅쓰고 in spite of danger

구해줍니다(구하다) to save, to rescue

존경합니다(존경하다) to respect

Grammar and Notes

Phrase

1. …자마자 (*as soon as*)

1) 불이 난 곳에 **닿자마자** 물을 뿌려서 불을 끕니다.
   As soon as they reach the place where the fire is, they spray water and extinguish the fire.
2) 집에서 **나오자마자** 비가 오기 시작했다.
   As soon as we came out of the house, it started to rain.
3) 집에 **오자마자** 나는 잠을 잤어요.
   As soon as I came home, I fell asleep.

2. … 무릅쓰고/불구하고 (*in spite of, at the risk of*)

1) 그는 부모의 반대를 **무릅쓰고** 그 여자와 결혼했다.
   He married that girl in spite of his parents' opposition.
2) 아저씨들이 위험을 **무릅쓰고** 일을 합니다.
   The men work in spite of the danger.

Developing Sentences

(Basic Form) (소방관들은) 구해줍니다. *Firefighters save.*

(How?) **위험을 무릅쓰고** 구해줍니다.

(When?) **사람이 있으면** 위험을 무릅쓰고 구해줍니다.

(Which people?) **불에서 미처 나오지 못한 사람이** 있으면, 위험을 무릅쓰고 구해줍니다.

(Final Sent.) *If there are people who could not yet come out, firefighters save them in spite of the danger.*

Translation

If a fire breaks out, the firefighters ride a fire truck and rush off. When a fire truck passes by, every car yields to them. As soon as they reach the place where the fire broke out, they spray water and extinguish the fire. If there are people who could not yet come out, the firefighters save them in spite of the danger. I respect the firefighters.

Classwork and Homework

1. Reading Comprehension: Answer these questions about the story.

   1) 불이 나면 누가 달려갑니까?

      | | | | 들이 달려가요.

   2) 뭐가 지나가면 차들이 길을 비켜줍니까?

      | | | |

   3) 소방관들은 무엇을 뿌려 불을 끕니까?

      | | 을 뿌려서 불을 꺼요.

   4) 불에서 나오지 못한 사람들을 누가 구해줍니까?

      | | | |

   5) 소방관 아저씨들은 어떻게 사람들을 구합니까?

      위험을 | | | | 구해줘요.

2. Translate these sentences into English.

   1) 수영장에 가자마자 물 속에 들어 갔어요.

      | |

   2) 집에 오자마자 숙제를 했어요.

      | |

   3) 군인들은 위험을 무릅쓰고 싸워요.

      | |

Let's Play Another Day, I'm Sick.

Achew! Hi. I'm sick. I... achew! Excuse me. I think I have a cold. I wasn't feeling good all day, but I still went to school. I wish I could play, but my head hurts too much. No running around for me today. Sorry. My mom said I should just go and lay in bed tonight. I don't know when I'll get better. I may not get better for a whole week. And do you know what that means? (·_<) No school! Achew!

46. 감기 (Cold)

머리가 아프고, 온몸이 피곤했습니다.

침대에 눕고 싶었습니다.

어머니께서는 감기 같다고 하시면서 약을

주셨습니다.

약을 먹고 자리에 누웠습니다.

입맛이 없어서 저녁도 먹지 않았습니다.

New Vocabulary

아프고 (아프다) to hurt, to be sick	피곤했습니다 to be tired
눕고 싶었습니다(눕고 싶다) to want to lie down	
감기 cold, flu	약 medicine
누웠습니다 (눕다) to lie down	입맛 appetite

Grammar and Notes

Phrase

1. …고 싶다 (*want to, wish*)

1) 나는 교수가 되고 **싶어요**. *I want to become a professor.*
2) 나는 컴퓨터를 사고 **싶어요**. *I want to buy a computer.*
3) 나는 수영을 하고 **싶어요**. *I want to swim.*

2. 같다 (*seem like*)

1) 감기 **같다**. *It seems like a cold.*
2) 누나는 꼭 가수 **같다**.
    My older sister seems just like a professional singer.
3) 너는 정말 천사 **같다**. *You really seem like an angel.*

3. 없어서 (*because I have no*)

1) 입맛이 **없어서** 저녁을 먹지 않았다.
    Because I did not have an appetite, I did not eat dinner.
2) 시계가 **없어서** 시간을 몰라요.
    Because I don't have a watch, I don't know the time.
3) 돈이 **없어서** 비싼 옷을 못 사요.
    Because I have no money, I can't buy expensive clothes.

4. …도 돼요? (*May I ...?*)

1) 이거 먹어**도 돼요?** *May I eat this?*
2) 이거 가져**도 돼요?** *May I have this?*
3) 밖에 나가**도 돼요?** *May I go outside?*

Translation

My head was hurting, and my entire body was tired. I wanted to lie down on my bed. My mother said that it seemed like a cold and gave me medicine. I took medicine and laid down in bed. Because I did not have an appetite, I did not even eat dinner.

1. Reading Comprehension: Answer these questions about the story.

   1) 코리는 어디가 아팠어요?

      ☐☐ 가 아팠어요.

   2) 코리는 어디에 눕고 싶다고 했어요?

      ☐☐ 에 눕고 싶다고 했어요.

   3) 코리 엄마는 무엇을 코리에게 주셨어요?

      ☐ 을 주셨어요.

   4) 코리는 무엇을 먹고 자리에 누웠어요?

      ☐ 을 먹고 누웠어요.

   5) 왜 코리는 저녁을 먹지 않았어요?

      ☐☐ 이 없어서 먹지 않았어요.

2. Translate these sentences into Korean.

   1) I want to become a teacher.

   2) I want to go to Paris.

   3) My sister seems like an angel.

   4) You seem like a baby.

Let's Learn How to Make More Money!

Today, I followed my mom to the bank. She said she had to withdraw some money. I think that means she went to take out money. I still don't understand exactly what happens at a bank. I don't get it. Is it a place where you can just go when you want to get money? I think they just give it to you, but I'm not sure. Wow, if that's true, then the bank just became my favorite place! Mom! Can we go to the bank again tomorrow? Do you know what a bank is for?

47. 저금 (Savings)

어머니께서는 작은 돈도 소중하게 모으십니다.

시장에서도 꼭 필요한 물건만 사십니다.

또 모든 물건을 아껴서 사용하십니다.

절약해서 모은 돈을 은행에 저금하십니다.

꾸준히 저금해서 큰돈을 만드십니다.

어머니는 참 알뜰하십니다.

New Vocabulary

돈 money	소중하게 valuably, carefully
꼭 surely, certainly	…만 only
아껴서 frugally	사용하십니다(사용하다) to use
절약해서(절약하다) to spare, to save	
저금 deposit	꾸준히 diligently
알뜰하십니다(알뜰하다) to be frugal	

Grammar and Notes

Phrase

1. ⋯만 (*only*)

Use 만 for emphasis.

1) 내 친구는 비싼 옷만 산다.
   My friend only buys expensive clothes.
2) 우리는 방학 때 놀기만 한다. *We only play during vacation.*
3) 아기는 잠만 자고 있다. *The baby only sleeps.*

2. ⋯해서 (*because*)

1) 나는 아파서 밥을 못 먹어요.
   I cannot have a meal because I am sick.
2) 늦어서 빨리 뛰어가야 해요.
   I have to run because I am late.
3) 피곤해서 일찍 자야 돼요.
   I have to go to bed early because I am tired.

3. ⋯해서 (*by (means of)*)

1) 절약해서 돈을 모으세요. *Save money by being frugal.*
2) 열심히 일해서 성공하세요. *Succeed by working hard.*
3) 노력해서 목적을 이루세요.
   Accomplish your goal by making an effort.

Grammar

Imperative Sentences

The tone of the sentence varies depending on the ending form.

Polite Tone   Verb stem + 세요: 조심해서 운전하세요. *Please drive carefully.*
Stern Tone   Verb stem + 시오: 저리로 가시오. *Go that way.*
Adult-to-child Tone   Verb stem + 라: 공부해라. 밥 먹어라. *Study. Eat meals.*

Translation

Mom carefully saves even small amounts of money. She only buys necessary things even at the market. Also, she uses everything frugally. She saves money and deposits it in the bank. She diligently deposits and turns it into big money. She lives frugally.

Classwork and Homework

1. Reading Comprehension: Answer these questions about the story.

   1) 누가 작은 돈도 소중하게 모읍니까?

   ☐☐☐ 께서 모아요.

   2) 어머니는 시장에서 어떤 물건만 삽니까?

   꼭 ☐☐ 한 물건만 사요.

   3) 어머니는 물건을 어떻게 사용합니까?

   ☐☐ 사용해요.

   4) 어머니는 절약해서 모은 돈을 어디에 저금합니까?

   ☐☐ 에 저금합니다.

2. Fill in the blanks using the ···만 expression.

   1) 아기가 <u>운다.</u> → 아기가 울기 ☐ 한다.

   2) 나는 <u>게임을</u> 해요. → 나는 게임 ☐ 해요.

   3) 누나는 <u>쇼핑을</u> 해요. → ☐

3. Match the phrases together to form a complete sentence.

   피곤해서 ◦   ◦ 성공하세요.

   노력해서 ◦   ◦ 약을 먹었어요.

   아파서 ◦   ◦ 쉬어야 해요.

Let's Think about the Future!

Have you ever thought about what you want to do in the future? Well, I haven't, but today I have to write a paragraph about what I want to do in the future for homework. Doesn't that stink? I should just tell the truth, that I want to be a superhero, Captain Kory! Well, actually I'll just write something my teacher would like... you know, that I want to be a doctor or a teacher or something. Heh heh....

48. 장래 희망 (Future Hope)

나는 장차 무슨 일을 하고 살까?

아픈 사람을 치료하는 의사가 될까?

학생들을 가르치는 선생님이 될까?

텔레비전에 나오는 뉴스 앵커가 될까?

나는 하고 싶은 일이 너무 많아요.

공부를 열심히 하면서 하나를 결정해야겠어요.

New Vocabulary

장차 later, in the future	치료하는(치료하다) to treat, to cure
의사 medical doctor	선생님 teacher
텔레비전 television	뉴스 앵커 news anchor
너무 too much	
결정해야겠어요(결정하다) to decide	

Grammar and Notes

Grammar

Interrogative Pronouns

To form an interrogative sentence (question):

1) Change the ending form from 다 to 까.

Predicate sentence	Interrogative sentence
학교에 갑니**다**.	학교에 갑니**까**?
운동을 합니**다**.	운동을 합니**까**?
여행을 합니**다**.	여행을 합니**까**?

2) Use the following interrogative pronouns:

누가 *who*　　언제 *when*　　왜 *why*
무엇 *what*　　어디 *where*　　어떻게 *how*

누가	**누가** 노래를 부를 수 있습니**까**? *Who can sing a song?*
무엇	누나는 **무엇을** 하고 있습니**까**? *What is my older sister doing?*
언제	**언제** 방학을 합니**까**? *When do you have vacation?*
어디	어머니는 **어디에** 계십니**까**? *Where is my mother?*
왜	**왜** 저기에 사람들이 모여 있습니**까**? *Why are people gathered over there?*
어떻게	이 전자 계산기를 **어떻게** 사용합니**까**? *How do you use this calculator?*

Translation

What kind of work will I do in the future? Will I become a doctor who treats sick people? Will I become a teacher who teaches students? Will I become a news anchor who is on television? I have too many things I want to do. While studying hard, I will have to decide on one.

Classwork and Homework

1. Reading Comprehension: Answer these questions about the story.

   1) 의사는 무엇을 합니까?

      ☐☐ 사람을 치료해요.

   2) 선생님은 무엇을 합니까?

      ☐☐ 을 가르쳐요.

   3) 텔레비전에는 누가 나옵니까?

      ☐☐ ☐☐ 가 나와요.

   4) 코리는 무슨 일이 너무 많습니까?

      ☐☐ ☐☐ 일이 너무 많아요.

2. Change the following sentences to the interrogative form.

   1) 누나는 학교에 갑니다.   ☐?

   2) 비가 옵니다.   ☐?

   3) 날씨가 춥습니다.   ☐?

3. Make a question using the interrogative word given.

   1) 누가? _____

   2) 언제? _____

   3) 왜? _____

Let's Learn about Doctors and Nurses!

My mom said I have to go to the hospital tomorrow for a checkup. I don't want to go. I think I'm very healthy. There's nothing wrong with me. What do they do during a checkup anyway? They're not going to give me a shot, are they? Or worse, I'm not going to have an operation, right? Ahh! Mom, I don't want to go to the hospital tomorrow! Oh, everyone gets a checkup? Even little babies? And it doesn't hurt? Well, maybe, it won't be so bad. But I still want to know more about what exeactly happens at the hospital.

49. 병원 (Hospital)

병원에 가면 의사가 환자를 치료합니다.

간호사는 의사를 도와 환자를 돌봅니다.

의사는 진찰을 한 후에 처방을 내립니다.

때로는 엑스레이도 찍고 입원시켜 치료합니다.

심한 경우 수술을 하기도 합니다.

New Vocabulary

환자 patient	간호사 nurse
돌봅니다(돌보다) to take care of	진찰 examination
처방 prescription	
내립니다(내리다) to give, to make out	
때로는 occasionally	엑스레이 x-ray
찍기도(찍다) to take (a picture, an x-ray)	
입원시켜(입원시키다) to hospitalize	
심한 경우 severe case	수술 surgery

Grammar and Notes

Phrase

1. …시키다 (*force, make*)

Ex. 입원시켜 (입원시키다)

1) 의사가 환자를 입원**시키다**.
   The doctor put the patient in the hospital.
2) 어머니는 딸에게 노래를 **시킨다**.
   Mom makes her daughter sing a song.
3) 아빠는 나에게 심부름을 **시켰다**.
   Dad made me run an errand.

2. Stem + ㄹ 경우 (*in case that*)

1) 비가 **올 경우**, 그 다음날 갑시다.
   In case that it rains, let's go the next day.
2) 내가 **늦을 경우**, 먼저 가세요.
   In case that I am late, go first.
3) 길이 **막힐 경우**, 좀 늦을 거예요.
   In case that the roads are backed up, I will be a little late.
4) **아플 경우**, 집에서 쉬세요.
   In case that you are sick, rest at home.

Vocabulary

Expressions for Sickness

1) 머리가 아파요. *My head hurts.*
2) 메스꺼워요. *I feel nauseated.*
3) 배가 아파요. *My stomach aches.*
4) 설사가 나요. *I have diarrhea.*
5) 어지러워요. *I feel dizzy.*
6) 열이 있어요. (열이 나요.) *I have a fever.*
7) 온몸이 아파요. *My entire body hurts.*
8) 이가 아파요. *My teeth ache.*

Translation

If you go to the hospital, the doctor treats the patient. The nurse helps the doctor and looks after the patient. After examining the patient, the doctor gives a prescription. Sometimes, he takes an x-ray and hospitalizes the patient for treatment. In severe cases, he performs surgery.

Classwork and Homework

1. Reading Comprehension: Answer these questions about the story.

    1) 아플 때에는 어디에 갑니까?

        ☐☐ 에 가요.

    2) 병원에서는 누가 환자를 치료합니까?

        ☐☐ 가 치료합니다.

    3) 간호사는 누구를 도와줍니까?

        ☐☐ 를 도와주어요.

    4) 의사는 언제 처방을 내려 줍니까?

        ☐☐ 을 한 후에 처방을 내려 주어요.

2. Change the sentences to the indicated form.

    Ex. 비가 온다.   ⟶   비가 올 경우

    1) 네가 아프다.   ⟶

    2) 날씨가 춥다.   ⟶

    3) 배가 고프다.   ⟶

3. How do you express these phrases in Korean?

    1) In case that your head hurts, go to the hospital.

    2) In case that your stomach aches, take some medicine.

Let's Thank Our Parents!

Tomorrow is my dad's birthday. I'm trying to think of what kind of present I should make for him. Maybe you can help me out? I want to make something really special this year. I haven't really listened to what my parents tell me to do. I want to show my parents that even though I goof off, I still love them. I'm very thankful that I have parents who take care of me like they do. I know! Maybe I can write something to let them know how important they are to me. How's this?

50. 부모 (Parents)

한국 사람들은 부모님을 소중히 여깁니다.
낳으시고 길러주신 사랑을 잊을 수 없습니다.
부모님은 언제나 자식을 위해 희생하시기
때문입니다. 그래서 부모님의 말씀을 잘
들어야 합니다. 훌륭하게 자라서 부모님을
기쁘게 해 드려야 합니다.

New Vocabulary

한국 사람 Korean

소중히 여깁니다(소중히 여기다) to think with care

낳으시고(낳다) to give birth   길러주신(길러주다) to raise

잊을 수 없습니다(잊을 수 없다) cannot forget

언제나 always, all the time   자식 child

희생하다 to sacrifice   들어야 합니다(듣다) to obey

훌륭하게(훌륭하다) to be honorable, to be admirable, to be great

기쁘게 해 드리다 to please

Grammar and Notes

1. …해야 한다, *must, have to*

1) 나는 오늘 저녁까지 숙제를 **마쳐야 한다**.
   I have to finish my homework by this evening.
2) 나는 4시까지 순이네 집에 **가야 한다**.
   I must go to Sooni's house by 4 o'clock.
3) 곧 **출발해야 합니다**. *We must leave soon.*

2. …해야만 한다, *must absolutely*

Note: 해야만 한다 **is a** stronger expression than 해야 한다.

1) 우리는 5시 비행기를 **타야만 합니다**.
   We must absolutely take the 5 o'clock flight.
2) 지금 출발해**야만 합니다**. *We must absolutely leave now.*
3) 그 일을 오늘밤까지 끝내**야만 합니다**.
   We must absolutely finish that work by tonight.

Developing Sentences

(Basic Form) (우리는) 기쁘게 해드려야 합니다.
We have to please.

(Whom?) (우리는) **부모님을** 기쁘게 해드려야 합니다.

(How?) (우리는) **훌륭하게 자라서** 부모님을 기쁘게 해드려야 합니다.

(Final sent.) *By growing up to be decent, we have to please our parents.*

Translation

Koreans think of their parents with care. They cannot forget the love with which their parents gave birth and raised them. It is because parents always sacrifice for their children. That is why we should obey their words. We have to grow up to be decent and please them.

Classwork and Homework

1. Reading Comprehension: Answer these questions about the story.

   1) 어떤 사람들이 부모를 소중히 여깁니까?

   | | | | | | 이 부모를 소중히 여겨요.

   2) 무슨 사랑을 잊을 수 없습니까?

   | | | | | | | | | 사랑

   3) 부모님은 누구를 위해 희생합니까?

   | | | 을 위해 희생해요.

   4) 누구의 말씀을 잘 들어야 합니까?

   | | | | 의 말씀

   5) 어떻게 부모님을 기쁘게 해드릴 수 있습니까?

   | | | | | 자라서

2. Change the sentences to the form shown below.

   Ex. 나는 약을 먹는다. → 나는 약을 <u>먹어야 한다</u>.

   1) 나는 숙제를 한다. →

   2) 아빠는 일하신다. →

3. Learn the Mother's Day song, "어머님 은혜."

   높고 높은 하늘이라 말들 하지만 / 나는 나는 높은 게 또 하나 있지
   낳으시고 기르시는 어머님 은혜 / 푸른 하늘 그보다도 높은 것 같애.

Answer

1. 가족 (Family)

1. Fill in the boxes with the correct conjunction. Use 와 or 과.

할아버지 | 와 | 할머니

코리 | 와 | 도로시

어머니 | 와 | 아버지

한국 | 과 | 미국

손 | 과 | 발

2. Match the word on the left with its meaning on the right.

가족 — sister
누나 — all
모두 — family
할아버지 — grandfather

3. On a separate sheet of paper, draw your family tree.

2. 인사 (Greeting)

❖ **Directions:** When people get together, they first exchange greetings to each other. Suppose you are a student and the other person is an adult. Match the correct greeting for each situation.

1. When you meet an adult,

You say to the adult, — "안녕."
The adult says to you, — "안녕하세요."

2. When you leave,

You say to the adult, — "안녕히 계세요."
The adult says to you, — "잘 가."

3. When the other person leaves,

You say to the adult, — "잘 있어."
The adult says to you, — "안녕히 가세요."

3. 집 (House)

1. Reading Comprehension: Answer these questions about the story.

   1) What are there in Kory's new house?
      There is a room, a kitchen, and a dining room.

   2) Is there a garage too?
      Yes, there is.

2. Fill in the blanks with the given word, using the phrase that means "there is/are."

   1) 집 | 집 | 이 | | 있 | 습 | 니 | 다 |.

   2) 식당 | 식 | 당 | 이 | | 있 | 습 | 니 | 다 |.

   3) 창고 | 창 | 고 | 가 | | 있 | 습 | 니 | 다 |.

3. Match each sentence with its meaning.

   1) 새집에는 부엌이 있어요. — We move to a new house.

   2) 텔레비전이 방에 있어요. — Grandmom is in the dining room.

   3) 우리는 새집으로 이사합니다. — There's a kitchen in the new house.

   4) 할머니는 식당에 있어요. — There is a television in the room.

4. 가구 (Furniture)

1. Using the words in the box below, fill in the blanks.

   방에, 벽에, 부엌에

   1) 어머니는 | 부 | 엌 | 에 | 가요. *Mom goes to the kitchen.*

   2) 그림이 | 벽 | 에 | 있어요. *The picture is on the wall.*

   3) 나는 | 방 | 에 | 있어요. *I am in the room.*

2. Change the sentences to the negative form.

   Ex. 시계가 있어요. *There is a watch.*
   → 시계가 없어요. *There is no watch.*

   1) 그림이 있어요.
      There is a picture.
      | 그 | 림 | 이 | | 없 | 어 | 요 |

   2) 소파가 있어요.
      There is a sofa.
      | 소 | 파 | 가 | | 없 | 어 | 요 |

   3) 누나는 방에 있어요. *My sister is in the room.*

      | 누 | 나 | 는 | | 방 | 에 | | 없 | 어 | 요 |

5. 몸 (Body)

1. Answer the following riddles.

   1) What is under your nose? 입

   2) What is on the side of your head? 귀

   3) What is at the bottom of your body? 발

2. Match the phrases to form a complete sentence.

   몸에는   눈이 있어요.

   얼굴에는   발이 있어요.

   다리에는   다리가 있어요.

3. Fill in the boxes with a correct conjunction. Use 와 or 과.

   눈 과 코   그림 과 시계

   다리 와 팔   소파 와 램프

   입 과 귀   침대 와 옷장

31

6. 아침 세수 (Morning Wash)

1. Put the correct subject particle (···은, ···는, ···이, ···가) or object particle (···을, ···를) in the boxes.

   1) 아버지 는/가 세수 를 합니다.

   2) 동생 은/이 옷 을 입습니다.

   3) 나 는 공부 를 합니다.

   4) 옷장 은/이 방에 있습니다.

   5) 누나 가 옵니다.

2. Match the words together to form the sentence on the right.

   할머니가   서로   입어요. — My sister wears the clothes.

   누나가   머리를   인사합니다. — We greet each other.

   우리는   옷을   빗습니다. — Grandma combs her hair.

35

7. 학교 (School)

1. Reading Comprehension: Answer these questions about the story.

   1) Where did they go? 학 교

   2) What did they do in school? 공 부

   3) With whom did they play? 친 구

2. Rearrange the words below to make a sentence.

   1) 학교에 가요 우리는   우 리 는   학 교 에   가 요

   2) 나는 공부해요 방에서   나 는   빙 에 시   공 부 해 요

   3) 옷을 누나는 입어요   누 나 는   옷 을   입 어 요

3. Let's learn more words about school. Copy the words below.

   teacher   desk   classroom

   선 생 님   책 상   교 실

   선 생 님   책 상   교 실

   homework   test/exam   English

   숙 제   시 험   영 어

   숙 제   시 험   영 어

39

8. 한국어 시간 (Korean Class)

1. Fill in the blanks to form the sentence on the left.

   1) I like this. 나 는 이 것 을 좋 아 해 요 .

   2) My sister likes that clothes (over there). 누 나 는 저/그 옷 을 좋 아 해 요 .

   3) This is a book. 이 것 은 책 입 니 다 .

   4) It is a picture. 저/그 것 은 사 진 입 니 다 .

2. Fill in the blanks using 이 and 저.

   1) This room 이 방   4) That window 저/그 창 문

   2) That house 저/그 집   5) This teacher 이 선 생 님

   3) This nose 이 코   6) That school 저/그 학 교

3. Match the questions with the correct answer.

   저분은 누구입니까? *Who is he?* — 책입니다.

   어디에 갑니까? *Where do you go?* — 오늘 갑니다.

   저것은 무엇입니까? *What is that?* — 우리 아빠입니다.

   언제 갑니까? *When do you go?* — 학교에 갑니다.

43

215

9. 심부름 (Errand)

1. Follow the model shown. Fill in the blanks using the words on the left.

   1) 아주머니 계세요?

     A) Grandfather   할 아 버 지 계 세 요 ?

     B) Someone (Hint: who)   누 구 계 세 요 ?

   2) 어머니가 이것을 보내셨어요.

     A) Father, book   아 버 지 가 책 을   보내셨어요.

     B) Teacher, sent   선 생 님 이 메모를 보 내 셨 어 요

     C) Grandmom, rice cake   할 머 니 가 떡 을   보내셨어요.

2. What expressions can you use in the following situations?

   1) Someone gave you a gift.   고 맙 습 니 다

   2) Your dad helped you with homework.   감 사 합 니 다

3. Describe a situation in which you might use these expressions.

    ◆실례합니다.   ◆미안합니다.

    when you need to   when you bump into
    move past someone in   them accidentally.
    a crowd.

47

10. 식사 I (Meal I)

1. Fill in the blanks to form the sentence on the left.

   1) I eat rice.   나 는 밥 을 먹 어 요 .

   2) My sister eats kimchi.   누 나 는 김 치 를 먹 어 요 .

   3) We eat bulgogi.   우 리 는 불 고 기 를 먹 어 요 .

2. Change the verb form from moderate to casual.

   1) 나는 먹습니다.   → 나는 먹 어 요

   2) 아빠는 이를 닦습니다.   → 아빠는 이를 닦 아 요

   3) 어머니는 옷을 입습니다. → 어머니는 옷을 입 어 요

3. Change the verbal form from moderate to plain.

   1) 나는 먹습니다.   → 나는 먹 는 다 .

   2) 아빠는 이를 닦습니다.   → 아빠는 이를 닦 는 다 .

   3) 어머니는 옷을 입습니다. → 어머니는 옷을 입 는 다 .

4. Ask your teacher or your mom about the following foods.

   잡채, 만두, 자장면, 국수, 갈비, 냉면, 비빔밥

51

11. 사계절 (Four Seasons)

1. Match the phrases together to form the sentence on the right.

   봄에는   열매가 익는다. *In the fall, fruits ripen.*

   여름에는   새싹이 나온다. *In the spring , buds come out.*

   가을에는   눈이 내린다. *In the winter, snow falls.*

   겨울에는   나무가 자란다. *In the summer, trees grow.*

2. Change the verb form from plain to casual.

   1) 열매가 익는다.   → 열 매 가 익 어 요 .

   2) 새싹이 나온다.   → 새 싹 이 나 와 요 .

   3) 눈이 내린다.   → 눈 이 내 려 요 .

   4) 나무가 자란다.   → 나 무 가 자 라 요 .

3. Name the season you see in the picture below.

   봄   여 름   가 을   겨 울

55

12. 옷 (Clothes)

1. What other equipments do you need for camping? Discuss it in class and write down some of them in Korean.

   물 통   손 전 등   비 상 약

   수 건   ……   ……

2. Use these words to fill in the blanks: 신어요, 써요, 입어요 and 껴요.

   1) 아빠는 모자를 써 요 .   2) 나는 바지를 입 어 요 .

   3) 누나는 속옷을 입 어 요 .   4) 할머니는 양말을 신 어 요 .

   5) 할아버지는 안경을 써 요 .   6) 엄마는 장갑을 껴 요 .

   7) 엄마는 구두를 신 어 요 .   8) 누나는 반지를 껴 요 .

3. Ask these questions to your classmates and write down their answers.

   1) 아침에 무엇을 입어요?   나는 티셔츠와 바지를 입어요.
     What do you wear in the morning?

   2) 아침에 무엇을 신어요?   나는 양말을 신어요.
     What do you wear in the morning?

59

13. 자연 (Nature)

1. Match the phrases to form a sentence.

산에는 ○   ○ 채소가 자랍니다.

골짜기에는 ○   ○ 파도가 출렁거립니다.

바다에는 ○   ○ 나무가 자랍니다.

들에는 ○   ○ 물이 흐릅니다.

2. Change the adjective to the modifier form.

Ex. 채소가 파랗다. → 파란 채소

1) 파도가 크다. → 큰 파도

2) 나무가 많다. → 많은 나무

3) 반찬이 맛있다. → 맛있는 반찬

3. What can you find or see...

1) in the mountains?   산에는 커다란 바위가 있습니다.

2) in the backyard?   뒷마당에는 예쁜 꽃이 피어 있습니다.

3) in the park?   공원에는 쉴 수 있는 의자가 많습니다.

63

14. 장난감 (Toys)

1. Fill in the blanks using the expression ···하고.

Ex. 나는 친구하고 학교에 가요.   *I go to school with my friend.*

1) 나는 아빠하고 산에 가요.   *I go to the mountain with dad.*

2) 누나는 친구하고 캠핑가요.   *My sister goes camping with her friend.*

3) 엄마는 누나하고 시장에 가요.   *Mom goes to the market with my sister.*

4) 캐티는 나하고 놀아요.   *Kathy plays with me.*

2. Combine the two sentences into one, using the expression ···고.

Ex. 나는 밥을 먹어요. 나는 놀아요.

→ 나는 밥을 먹고 놀아요.

1) 나무가 크다. 나무가 푸르다.

→ 나무가 크고 푸르다.

2) 바다는 넓다. 파도가 출렁거린다.

→ 바다는 넓고 파도가 출렁거린다.

3) 우리는 공부해요. 우리는 놀아요.

→ 우리는 공부하고 놀아요.

67

15. 운동 (Sports)

1. Reading Comprehension: Answer these questions about the story.

1) 학생들이 언제 운동을 합니까?

공부를 마치고 (운동을 합니다).

2) 가을에는 무슨 운동을 합니까?

풋볼 (야구, 풋볼, 농구)

3) 겨울에는 무슨 운동을 합니까?

수영 (레슬링, 농구, 수영, 스키)

4) 봄에는 무슨 운동을 합니까?

테니스 (테니스, 축구, 배구)

5) 어떤 운동이 공을 사용하지 않습니까?

볼링, 농구, 야구, 탁구, 축구, 수영, 배구, 골프, 레슬링

2. Ask these questions to your classmates.

1) 무슨 운동을 합니까? *What sport do you play?*

A) 나는 축구를 합니다. *I play soccer.*

B) 나는 수영을 합니다. *I swim.*

2) 무슨 운동을 좋아합니까? *What sport do you like?*

A) 나는 수영을 좋아합니다. *I like swimming.*

B) 나는 테니스를 좋아합니다. *I like to play tennis.*

71

16. 숫자 (Numbers)

1. Reading Comprehension: Answer these questions about the story.

1) 아기 돼지들이 무엇을 건넙니까?

시냇물 (시냇물, 강, 들)

2) 아기 돼지들이 왜 야단을 했습니까?

A) 배가 고파서 *because they were hungry*

B) 길을 몰라서 *because they were lost*

C) 한 마리가 없다고 *that there was one missing*

2. Fill in the blanks with the correct number.

하나, 둘, 셋, 넷, 다섯, 여섯,

일곱, 여덟, 아홉, 열, 열하나

3. Count how many are in the picture and write down the answer.

네 권   세 사람   두 개   열 장

75

217

17. 색깔 (Colors)

1. Reading Comprehension: Answer these questions about the story.

1) 하늘에는 무엇이 보입니까?

무 지 개 가 보입니다. .

2) 언제 무지개가 하늘에 나타났습니까?

소 나 기 가 온 뒤에 (나타났어요).

3) 무지개에서 무슨 색을 찾을 수 없습니까?

흰 색 과 검 은 색

2. Match the names of the colors corresponding with each other.

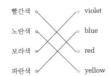

빨간색 —— violet
노란색 —— blue
보라색 —— red
파란색 —— yellow

3. Can you name the seven colors of the rainbow?

빨 간 색 주 황 색 노 란 색 초 록 색

파 란 색 남 색 보 라 색

79

18. 피아노 연습 (Piano Practice)

1. Reading Comprehension: Answer these questions about the story.

1) 오늘 누가 오십니까?

피 아 노 선생님 (이 오십니다).

2) 코리는 피아노 연습을 어떻게 합니까?

열 심 히 합니다.

3) 손가락이 건반 위에서 어떻게 움직입니까?

바 쁘 게 움직입니다.

2. Change the adjectives to the adverb form.

1) 바쁘다 → 바 쁘 게

2) 맛있다 → 맛 있 게

3) 아름답다 → 아 름 답 게

83

19. 부엌 (Kitchen)

1. Reading Comprehension: Answer these questions about the story.

1) 식사를 한 후 어머니는 무엇을 합니까? *What does the mother do after a meal?*

그 릇 을 씻어요.

2) 수납장에는 무엇이 있습니까? *What things are in the cabinet?*

접 시 컵 냄 비 가 있어요.

3) 서랍에는 무엇이 있습니까? *What things are in the drawer?*

수 저 포 크 나 이 프 가 있어요.

4) 냉장고에는 무엇이 있어요? *What is in the refrigerator?*

맛 있 는 음식이 있어요.

2. Match the phrases together to form a complete sentence.

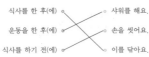

식사를 한 후(에) —— 샤워를 해요.
운동을 한 후(에) —— 손을 씻어요.
식사를 하기 전(에) —— 이를 닦아요.

87

20. 시내 (Downtown)

1. Reading Comprehension: Answer these questions about the story.

1) 시내는 얼마나 복잡합니까?

매 우 복잡해요.

2) 높은 건물에는 무엇이 있습니까?

상 점 과 사 무 실 이 있어요.

3) 시내에 갈 때 무엇을 타면 편리합니까?

지 하 철 을 타면 편리해요.

2. Change the sentence to a when-clause using the …때 phrase.

1) 식사를 한다. → 식사를 할 때

2) 학교에 간다. → 학 교 에 갈 때

3) 여름이 온다. → 여 름 이 올 때

3. Change the sentence to an if-clause using the …면 phrase.

1) 운동을 하다 → 운동을 하 면

2) 공부를 하다 → 공부를 하 면

4. Change the words from singular to plural form.

1) 사람 사 람 들 2) 상점 상 점 들 3) 차 차 들

91

218

21. 동네 (Community)

1. Reading Comprehension: Answer these questions about the story.

   1) 코리의 동네는 어떻습니까?

      | 살 | 기 | 에 | 좋습니다.

   2) 호숫가에는 무엇이 있습니까?

      | 산 | 책 | 길 | 이 있습니다.

   3) 집 가까이 무엇이 있습니까?

      | 시 | 장 | 이 있습니다.

2. Fill in the blank with the correct conjunction, 와 or 과.

   1) 시장 | 과 | 집   2) 학교 | 와 | 호수

   3) 도서관 | 과 | 병원   4) 상점 | 과 | 사무실

3. Answer the questions using the verbs given below.

   1) 왜 학교에 못 갑니까? *Why can't you go to school?* (아프다)

      | 아 | 프 | 기 때문에 학교에 못 가요.

   2) 왜 수영을 합니까? *Why do you swim?* (덥다)

      | 덥 | 기 | 때문에 수영을 해요.

95

22. 학용품 (School Supplies)

1. Reading Comprehension: Answer these questions about the story.

   1) 무엇이 거의 끝났습니까?

      | 방 | 학 | 이 거의 끝났어요.

   2) 코리는 왜 문구점으로 갔습니까?

      학용품을 | 사 | 기 | 위 | 해 | 서 | 갔어요.

   3) 책가방은 누가 사 주셨습니까?

      | 어 | 머 | 니 | 께서 사 주셨어요.

2. Change the sentences from the present tense to the past tense.

   1) 나는 학교에 간다. → 나는 학교에 | 갔 | 다 |.

   2) 누나는 노트를 산다. → 누나는 노트를 | 샀 | 다 |.

   3) 우리는 운동을 한다. → 우리는 운동을 | 했 | 다 |.

3. Fill in the blanks using the …하기 위해서 phrase.

   1) 왜 학교에 갔습니까?

      공부 | 하 | 기 | 위 | 해 | 서 | 학교에 갔어요.

   2) 왜 시장에 갔습니까?

      물건을 | 사 | 기 | 위 | 해 | 서 | 시장에 갔어요.

99

23. 과일 (Fruit)

1. Reading Comprehension: Answer these questions about the story.

   1) 코리는 누구를 따라 시장에 갔습니까?

      | 어 | 머 | 니 | 를 | 따 | 라 | 시장에 갔어요.

   2) 과일 상점에는 무슨 과일이 가득 쌓여 있었습니까?

      | 사 | 과 |, | 수 | 박 |, | 딸 | 기 |, | 포 | 도 |

      | 바 | 나 | 나 | 등이 가득 쌓여 있었어요.

   3) 채소 시장에는 무슨 야채들이 있었습니까?

      | 오 | 이 |, | 감 | 자 |, | 파 |, | 배 | 추 | 가 있었어요.

2. Match the present tense verb form with its past tense form.

   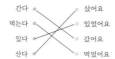

   간다 — 샀어요
   먹는다 — 있었어요
   있다 — 갔어요
   산다 — 먹었어요

3. Change the sentences into the past tense form.

   1) 시장에는 배추가 있습니다.

      시장에는 배추가 | 있 | 었 | 습 | 니 | 다 |

   2) 어머니는 야채를 삽니다.

      어머니는 야채를 | 샀 | 습 | 니 | 다 |

103

24. 토끼와 거북이 (Tortoise & Hare)

1. Reading Comprehension: Answer these questions about the story.

   1) 누가 경주합니까?

      | 거 | 북 | 이 | 와 | 토 | 끼 | 가 경주해요.

   2) 토끼와 거북이 중 누가 더 빠릅니까?

      | 토 | 끼 | 가 더 빨라요.

   3) 거북이는 어떻게 기어갔습니까?

      | 쉬 | 지 | 않 | 고 | 기어갔어요.

   4) 누가 경주에서 이겼습니까?

      | 거 | 북 | 이 | 가 이겼어요.

2. Fill in the blanks with the appropriate expressions.

   1) 토끼는 거북이 | 보 | 다 | 더 | 빨라요.

      The hare runs faster than the tortoise.

   2) 누나는 나 | 보 | 다 | 더 | 커요. *My sister is taller than me.*

   3) 거북이는 쉬지 | 않 | 고 | 기어갑니다. *The tortoise crawls without resting.*

   4) 나는 놀지 | 않 | 고 | 공부해요. *I study without playing.*

   5) 거북이는 | 느 | 리 | 지 | 만 | 쉬지 않고 기어갑니다.

      Even though the tortoise is slow, it crawls without resting.

107

25. 도서관 (Library)

1. Reading Comprehension: Answer these questions about the story.

1) 코리는 어디에 갔습니까?

도 서 관 에 갔어요.

2) 도서관에는 무슨 책이 있습니까?

사 전 , 전 기 , 소 설 , 잡 지 책이 있어요.

3) 도서관에서 사람들이 무엇을 하고 있습니까?

소리 없이 책 을 읽고 있어요.

4) 코리는 무슨 책을 읽었습니까?

동 화 책 을 읽었어요.

2. Change the sentences to the negative form using 없, 안, or 못.

1) 사람이 있어요. →(there isn't)→ 사람이 없 어 요 .

책이 있습니다. → 책이 없 습 니 다 .

2) 나는 학교에 갑니다. →(not)→ 나는 학교에 안 갑 니 다

우리는 공부를 해요. → 우리는 공부를 안 해 요 .

3) 나는 책을 읽어요. →(cannot)→ 나는 책을 못 읽 어 요 .

코리는 수영을 해요. → 코리는 수영을 못 해 요 .

111

26. 청소 (Cleaning)

1. Reading Comprehension: Answer these questions about the story.

1) 아버지는 매일 아침 무엇을 합니까?

골 목 청 소 를 하세요.

2) 골목이 왜 지저분합니까?

종 이 , 빈 깡 통 , 낙 엽 때문에 지저분해요.

3) 오늘은 누가 더 나왔습니까?

나 하고 이 웃 집 아저씨도 나왔어요.

2. Fill in the blanks with the ···면서 phrase.

1) 우리는 웃으 면 서 청소했어요. *We cleaned as we laughed.*

2) 모두 이야기하 면 서 밥을 먹어요. *All eat the meal while talking.*

3) 우리는 이야기하 면 서 걸어갔어요. *We walked as we talked.*

3. Change the words into the plural form.

1) 너 너 희   2) 아저씨 아 저 씨 들

3) 나 우 리   4) 당신 당 신 들

5) 깡통 깡 통 들   6) 낙엽 낙 엽 들

115

27. 눈사람 (Snowman)

1. Reading Comprehension: Answer these questions about the story.

1) 언제 눈이 내렸습니까?

어 젯 밤 에 눈이 내렸어요.

2) 누가 눈사람을 만들었습니까?

나 하고 누 나 가 눈사람을 만들었어요.

3) 눈사람에게 무엇을 붙였습니까?

눈 , 눈 썹 , 코 , 입 을 붙였어요.

4) 머리에는 무엇을 씌웠습니까?

모 자 를 씌웠어요.

2. Fill in the blanks using 도 (*even, too, also*).

1) 엄마는 시장에 가요. 나 도 시장에 가요.
Mom goes to the market. I also go to the market.

2) 엄마는 옷을 입어요. 누나 도 옷을 입어요.
Mom puts on clothes. My sister also puts on clothes.

3) 나는 영어를 배워요. 한국어 도 배워요.
I learn English. I learn Korean too.

4) 나는 축구를 해요. 나는 수영 도 해요.
I play soccer. I swim too.

119

28. 달 (Months)

1. Reading Comprehension: Answer these questions about the story.

1) 어디에 달력이 있습니까?

벽 에 달력이 있어요.

2) 1년에는 몇 달이 있습니까?

1 2 달이 있어요.

3) 1년에는 모두 몇 일이 있습니까?

3 6 5 일이 있어요.

4) 3월에는 누구의 생일이 있습니까?

엄 마 의 생 신 이 있어요.

5) 코리는 생일날에 무슨 표를 했습니까?

동 그 라 미 표를 그렸어요.

2. Fill in the blanks using the possessive particle ···의.

1) 엄마 의 생신   2) 아빠 의 생신

3) 누나 의 옷   4) 할아버지 의 모자

123

29. 식사 2 (Meal 2)

1. Reading Comprehension: Answer these questions about the story.

1) 밥상에 무엇이 가득합니까?

밥 과 반 찬 이 가득해요.

2) 모두 어디에 둘러앉았습니까?

모두 밥 상 에 둘러앉았어요.

3) 음식이 얼마나 맛있습니까?

참 맛있어요.

4) 모두 어떻게 식사합니까?

맛 있 게 식사해요.

2. Translate these sentences into Korean.

1) Can I have a little more rice? | 밥을 조금 더 주세요.
2) The food is delicious. | 음식이 맛있어요.
3) It is hot. | 뜨거워요.
4) It is too spicy. | 너무 매워요.
5) What tastes good? | 무엇이 맛있어요?

127

30. 쇼핑 (Shopping)

1. Reading Comprehension: Answer these questions about the story.

1) 누나는 누구하고 쇼핑을 갔습니까?

엄 마 하고 갔어요.

2) 상점에는 무엇이 많아요?

예 쁜 옷 들이 많아요.

3) 누나는 무슨 치마를 골랐습니까?

빨 간 치마를 골랐어요.

4) 구두와 치마 값이 모두 얼마였습니까?

4 7 달러 5 0 센트였어요.

5) 누나는 엄마에게 뭐라고 말했습니까?

고 맙 다 고 말했어요.

2. Ask and Answer the following questions with your friends.

1) When you want to eat some food, where do you go? | 식당에 가요.
2) When you want to buy a book, where do you go? | 서점에 가요.
3) When you need to buy clothes, where do you go? | 옷 가게에 가요.

131

31. 동물원 (Zoo)

1. Reading Comprehension: Answer these questions about the story.

1) 코리네 가족은 어디에 갔습니까?

동 물 원 에 갔어요.

2) 동물원에는 무슨 동물들이 있었습니까?

사 자 , 호 랑 이 , 원 숭 이 , 곰 등이 있어요.

3) 점심때 무엇을 먹었습니까?

김 밥 을 먹었어요.

4) 김밥은 누가 만들었습니까?

어 머 니 가 만들었어요

2. Fill in the blanks with the correct words.

코 끼 리   호 랑 이

3. Change the sentences to a participial phrase.

1) 어머니가 김밥을 만들었다. → 어머니가 만 든 김밥

2) 우리 안에 동물들이 있다. → 우리 안에 있 는 동물

135

32. 시장 (Market)

1. Reading Comprehension: Answer these questions about the story.

1) 시장은 무엇으로 붐볐습니까?

사 람 들로 붐볐습니다.

2. Match the words together to form a participial phrase.

물건 값을   하는 사람

포장을   고르는 사람

물건을   묻는 사람

3. Change the sentences to a participial phrase.

Ex. 사람들이 인사합니다. → 인 사 하 는 사람들

1) 학생들이 공부합니다. → 공 부 하 는 학생들

2) 사람들이 일합니다. → 일 하 는 사람들

3) 학생들이 운동을 합니다. → 운동을 하 는 학생들

139

33. 해와 달과 별 (Sun, Moon & Star)

1. Reading Comprehension: Answer these questions about the story.

1) 하늘에는 무엇이 빛납니까?

| 해 | 가 빛나요.

2) 밤하늘에는 무엇이 반짝입니까?

| 수 | 많 | 은 | | 별 | 이 반짝여요.

3) 무엇이 뜨면 밤도 낮처럼 밝습니까?

| 둥 | 근 | | 달 | 이 뜨면 밝아요.

4) 무엇 때문에 시골 마을이 아름답습니까?

| 달 | 빛 | 때문에 아름다워요.

2. Match the phrases together to form a complete sentence.

비가 오면 ○ ○ 수많은 별이 반짝입니다.

공부를 열심히 하면 ○ ○ 소풍을 못 가요.

밤이 되면 ○ ○ 성적이 올라가요.

3. Translate these sentences into Korean.

1) You cry like a baby. 아기처럼 울어요.

2) My sister speaks like an adult. 누나는 어른처럼 말해요.

3) Today is warm like spring. 오늘은 봄처럼 따뜻합니다.

143

34. 전화 (Telephone)

1. Reading Comprehension: Answer these questions about the story.

1) 따르릉 소리를 내며 무엇이 왔습니까?

| 전 | 화 | 가 왔어요.

2) 누가 전화를 받았습니까?

| 누 | 나 | 가 전화를 받았어요.

3) 누나가 무슨 말을 처음 했습니까?

| 여 | 보 | 세 | 요 | 라고 말했어요.

4) 누구를 찾는 전화였습니까?

| 엄 | 마 | 를 찾는 전화였어요.

2. Put the following telephone dialogue in order.

언제쯤 돌아오나요? | 3 |

안녕히 계세요. | 4 |

여보세요? | 1 |

순이 좀 바꿔 주세요. | 2 |

147

35. 요일 (Day)

1. Reading Comprehension: Answer these questions about the story.

1) 일주일에는 몇 일이 있습니까?

| 7 | 일이 있어요.

2) 대부분의 사람들이 언제부터 언제까지 일합니까?

| 월 | 요 | 일 | 부터 | 금 | 요 | 일 | 까지 일해요.

3) 사람들이 언제 쉽니까?

| 주 | 말 | 에 쉽니다.

4) 한국 학교에서는 언제 한국어를 공부합니까?

| 토 | 요 | 일 | 에 공부합니다.

2. Fill in the blanks with the correct name of the day.

1) Monday | 월 | 요 | 일 | 2) Wednesday | 수 | 요 | 일 |

3) Friday | 금 | 요 | 일 | 4) Sunday | 일 | 요 | 일 |

3. Complete the sentences using a proper phrase.

1) 여기서 | 부 | 터 | 학교 | 까 | 지 | 얼마나 멀어요?

How far is it from here to school?

2) 나는 아침 | 부 | 터 | 저녁 | 까 | 지 | 일했어요.

I worked from morning till evening.

151

36. 생일 (Birthday)

1. Reading Comprehension: Answer these questions about the story.

1) 오늘은 누구의 생신입니까?

| 할 | 아 | 버 | 지 | 의 생신입니다.

2) 누가 부엌에서 음식을 만듭니까?

| 어 | 머 | 니 | 와 | 고 | 모 |

3) 할아버지의 생신에 누가 모였습니까?

| 친 | 척 | 들이 다 모였습니다.

4) 할아버지께 무엇을 드렸습니까?

| 선 | 물 | 을 드렸습니다.

2. Change the following words and sentences to the honorific form.

1) 할아버지가 → 할아버지 | 께 | 서 |

2) 할머니가 → 할머니 | 께 | 서 |

3) 아버지가 → 아버지 | 께 | 서 |

4) 할아버지가 온다. → 할아버지 | 께 | 서 | | 오 | 신 | 다 |

5) 할머니가 간다. → 할머니 | 께 | 서 | | 가 | 신 | 다 |

6) 아버지가 일한다. → 아버지 | 께 | 서 | | 일 | 하 | 신 | 다 |

155

222

37. 군인 (Soldier)

1. Reading Comprehension: Answer these questions about the story.

   1) 군인들이 무엇을 지킵니까?

      나 라 를 지켜요.

   2) 육군은 어디에서 나라를 지킵니까?

      육 지 에서 나라를 지켜요.

   3) 해군은 어디에서 나라를 지킵니까?

      바 다 에서 나라를 지킵니다.

   4) 군인들은 왜 나라를 지킵니까?

      우리가 편 안 하게 살도록 나라를 지킵니다.

2. Change these sentences into the negative form.

   1) 나는 스키를 탑니다. 나는 스키를 타 지 못합니다. (cannot)

   2) 누나는 피아노를 칩니다. 누나는 피아노를 치 지 못합니다. (cannot)

   3) 우리는 싸움을 합니다. 우리는 싸움을 하지 않 습 니 다 (not)

   4) 나는 거짓말을 합니다. 나는 거짓말을 하지 않 습 니 다 (not)

   5) 소리가 납니다. 소리가 안 납 니 다 (not)

159

38. 바닷가 (Beach)

1. Reading Comprehension: Answer these questions about the story.

   1) 바다는 얼마나 넓습니까?

      참 넓어요.

   2) 파도는 해변에서 어떻게 부서집니까?

      하 얗 게 부서집니다.

   3) 모래밭에는 어떤 사람들이 많습니까?

      검 게 탄 사람들이 많아요.

   4) 아이들이 무엇을 만들고 있습니까?

      모 래 성 을 만들고 있어요.

2. Look at the pictures. What are they doing?

   1) 수 영 을 하고 있습니다.   2) 공 부 를 하고 있습니다.

   3) 야 구 를 하고 있습니다.   4) 노 래 를 하고 있습니다.

163

39. 결심 (Resolution)

1. Reading Comprehension: Answer these questions about the story.

   1) 코리는 어떤 결심을 합니까?

      새 로 운 결심을 해요.

   2) 코리는 지난해보다 무엇을 더 열심히 하려고 합니까?

      공 부 를 열심히 하려고 해요.

   3) 코리는 누구의 말씀을 잘 들으려고 합니까?

      부 모 님 말씀을 잘 들으려고 해요.

   4) 날마다 무엇을 쓰려고 합니까?

      일 기 를 쓰려고 해요.

   5) 누구와 사이 좋게 지내려고 합니까?

      친 구 들 과 사이 좋게 지내려고 해요.

2. Change the sentences into the future tense form.

   1) 나는 교수가 된다. → 나는 교수가 될 것이다.

   2) 나는 부자가 된다. → 나는 부자가 될 것이다.

   3) 나는 일기를 쓴다. → 나는 일기를 쓸 것이다.

   4) 비가 온다. → 비가 올 것이다.

167

40. 가정 (Home)

1. Reading Comprehension: Answer these questions about the story.

   1) 아버지는 어디에 가십니까?

      회 사 에 가세요.

   2) 코리와 누나는 어디에 갑니까?

      학 교 에 가요.

   3) 어머니는 어디에서 일하십니까?

      집 에서 일하세요.

   4) 식구들이 언제 집으로 돌아옵니까?

      저 녁 이 되면 집으로 돌아와요.

2. Change the following words and sentences to the honorific form.

   1) 아버지 아 버 님   2) 교수 교 수 님

   3) 어머니 어 머 님   4) 박사 박 사 님

   5) 신생 선 생 님   6) 감독 감 독 님

   7) 할아버지가 있다. → 할아버지께서 계신다.

   8) 할머니가 잔다. → 할머니께서 주무신다.

   9) 아버지가 온다. → 아버지께서 오신다.

171

223

41. 손님 (Guest)

1. Reading Comprehension: Answer these questions about the story.

1) 누가 코리네 집을 방문했습니까?

아빠의 [친][구] 가족이 방문했어요.

2) 누가 손님들에게 집을 안내했습니까?

[엄][마] 가 하셨어요.

3) 내일은 모두 어디로 가기로 했습니까?

[시][내][구][경] 을 가기로 했어요.

4) 누가 밤 늦게까지 이야기를 했습니까?

[어][른][들] 이 하셨습니다.

2. Fill in the blanks with a correct object particle (을, 를, 에게).

1) 나는 숙제 [를] 했어요.

2) 아빠는 나 [에][게] 장난감 [을] 사 주셨어요.

3) 우리는 누나 [에][게] 선물 [을] 사 주었어요.

3. Match the words together to make a complete sentence.

12시까지 ——— 오세요.

공부하는 동안 ⤬ 갈게요.

점심때까지 ⤬ 조용히 하세요.

175

42. 날씨 (Weather)

1. Reading Comprehension: Answer these questions about the story.

1) 비가 오기 전에 날씨가 어떠했습니까?

[무][척] 더웠습니다.

2) 비구름이 어느 쪽에서 몰려왔습니까?

[서][쪽] 에서 몰려왔습니다.

3) 비구름이 몰려오니 하늘이 어떻게 변했습니까?

하늘이 [어][두][워] 졌습니다.

4) 소나기가 오니까 날씨가 어떻게 변했습니까?

갑자기 [시][원] 해졌습니다.

5) 이런 여름 날씨를 뭐라고 합니까?

[변][덕] 스럽다고 합니다.

2. Fill in the banks by choosing the right adverb from the word bank.

1) 거북이는 [너][무] 느리다.   너무

2) 아빠가 [아][직] 안 오셨어요.   꼭

3) 12시까지 [꼭] 오세요.   빨리

4) 늦지 않도록 [빨][리] 가세요.   아직

179

43. 명절 (Holiday)

1. Reading Comprehension: Answer these questions about the story.

1) 추석은 언제부터 내려오는 명절입니까?

[옛][날] 부터 내려오는 명절이에요.

2) 이날은 무엇으로 음식을 만들어 먹습니까?

[새][곡][식] 으로 음식을 만들어 먹어요.

3) 추석에 모인 가족들은 누구를 기억합니까?

[조][상] 을 기억해요.

4) 이날은 가족들이 어디서도 옵니까?

[멀][리] 서도 와요.

5) 누가 추석을 기다립니까?

[모][두] 가 기다립니다.

2. Fill in the blanks with the correct preposition (로, 으로).

1) 아빠는 비행기 [로] 한국에 가요.

2) 엄마는 펜 [으][로] 편지를 써요.

3) 나는 수건 [으][로] 차를 닦아요.

4) 할머니는 배추 [로] 김치를 만들어요.

183

44. 시간 (Time)

1. Reading Comprehension: Answer these questions about the story.

1) 코리는 몇 시에 일어납니까?

아침 [6]시 [3][0] 분에 일어나요.

2) 학교에는 어떻게 갑니까?

[버][스] 로 가요.

3) 8시 15분에 뭐가 시작됩니까?

[수][업] 이 시작되요.

4) 점심은 어디에서 먹습니까?

[식][당] 에서 먹어요.

5) 학교는 몇 시에 끝납니까?

[2]시 [3][0] 분에 끝나요.

6) 집에 오면 무엇을 먼저 합니까?

[숙][제] 를 먼저 해요.

7) 잠들기 전에 무엇을 합니까?

[책] 을 읽어요.

2. Ask these questions to your classmates.

1) 몇 시에 일어납니까? *What time do you get up?* 아침 7시에 일어납니다.

2) 몇 시에 학교에 갑니까? *What time do you go to school?* 7시 50분에 학교에 갑니다.

3) 몇 시에 잡니까? *What time do you go to bed?* 밤 10시 30분에 잡니다.

187

45. 소방관 (Firefighter)

1. Reading Comprehension: Answer these questions about the story.

1) 불이 나면 누가 달려갑니까?

소 방 관 들이 달려가요.

2) 뭐가 지나가면 차들이 길을 비켜줍니까?

소 방 차 가 지나가면 차들이 길을 비켜줘요.

3) 소방관들은 무엇을 뿌려 불을 끕니까?

물 을 뿌려서 불을 꺼요.

4) 불에서 나오지 못한 사람들을 누가 구해줍니까?

소 방 관 이 구해줘요.

5) 소방관 아저씨들은 어떻게 사람들을 구합니까?

위험을 **무 릅 쓰 고** 구해줘요.

2. Translate these sentences into English.

1) 수영장에 가자마자 물 속에 들어 갔어요.

As soon as I went to the swimming pool, I went into the water.

2) 집에 오자마자 숙제를 했어요.

As soon as I came home, I did my homework.

3) 군인들은 위험을 무릅쓰고 싸워요.

The soldiers fought in spite of danger.

191

46. 감기 (Cold)

1. Reading Comprehension: Answer these questions about the story.

1) 코리는 어디가 아팠어요?

머 리 가 아팠어요.

2) 코리는 어디에 눕고 싶다고 했어요?

침 대 에 눕고 싶다고 했어요.

3) 코리 엄마는 무엇을 코리에게 주셨어요?

약 을 주셨어요.

4) 코리는 무엇을 먹고 자리에 누웠어요?

약 을 먹고 누웠어요.

5) 왜 코리는 저녁을 먹지 않았어요?

입 맛 이 없어서 먹지 않았어요.

2. Translate these sentences into Korean.

1) I want to become a teacher. | 나는 선생님이 되고 싶어요.

2) I want to go to Paris. | 나는 파리에 가고 싶어요.

3) My sister seems like an angel. | 누나는 천사 같다.

4) You seem like a baby. | 너는 아기 같다.

195

47. 저금 (Savings)

1. Reading Comprehension: Answer these questions about the story.

1) 누가 작은 돈도 소중하게 모읍니까?

어 머 니 께서 모아요.

2) 어머니는 시장에서 어떤 물건만 삽니까?

꼭 **필 요** 한 물건만 사요.

3) 어머니는 물건을 어떻게 사용합니까?

아 껴 서 사용해요.

4) 어머니는 절약해서 모은 돈을 어디에 저금합니까?

은 행 에 저금합니다.

2. Fill in the blanks using the …만 expression.

1) 아기가 운다. → 아기가 울기 **만** 한다.

2) 나는 게임을 해요. → 나는 게임 **만** 해요.

3) 누나는 쇼핑을 해요. → **누나는 쇼핑만 해요.**

3. Match the phrases together to form a complete sentence.

피곤해서 ——— 성공하세요.

노력해서 ——— 약을 먹었어요.

아파서 ——— 쉬어야 해요.

199

48. 장래희망 (Future Hope)

1. Reading Comprehension: Answer these questions about the story.

1) 의사는 무엇을 합니까?

아 픈 사람을 치료해요.

2) 선생님은 무엇을 합니까?

학 생 을 가르쳐요.

3) 텔레비전에는 누가 나옵니까?

뉴 스 앵 커 가 나와요.

4) 코리는 무슨 일이 너무 많습니까?

하 고 싶 은 일이 너무 많아요.

2. Change the following sentences to the interrogative form.

1) 누나는 학교에 갑니다. | 누나는 학교에 갑니까 | ?

2) 비가 옵니다. | 비가 옵니까 | ?

3) 날씨가 춥습니다. | 날씨가 춥습니까 | ?

3. Make a question using the interrogative word given.

1) 누가? **누가 학교에 갑니까?**

2) 언제? **언제 비가 옵니까?**

3) 왜? **왜 날씨가 춥습니까?**

203

49. 병원 (Hospital)

1. Reading Comprehension: Answer these questions about the story.

1) 아플 때에는 어디에 갑니까?

   병 원 에 가요.

2) 병원에서는 누가 환자를 치료합니까?

   의 사 가 치료합니다.

3) 간호사는 누구를 도와줍니까?

   의 사 를 도와주어요.

4) 의사는 언제 처방을 내려 줍니까?

   진 찰 을 한 후에 처방을 내려 주어요.

2. Change the sentences to the indicated form.

Ex. 비가 온다.　→　비가 올 경우

1) 네가 아프다.　→　네가 아플 경우

2) 날씨가 춥다.　→　날씨가 추울 경우

3) 배가 고프다.　→　배가 고플 경우

3. How do you express these phrases in Korean?

1) In case that your head hurts, go to the hospital.

   머리가 아플 경우, 병원에 가세요.

2) In case that your stomach aches, take some medicine.

   배가 아플 경우, 약을 드세요.

207

50. 부모 (Parents)

1. Reading Comprehension: Answer these questions about the story.

1) 어떤 사람들이 부모를 소중히 여깁니까?

   한 국 사 람 들 이 부모를 소중히 여겨요.

2) 무슨 사랑을 잊을 수 없습니까?

   낳 으 시 고 길 러 주 신 사랑

3) 부모님은 누구를 위해 희생합니까?

   자 식 을 위해 희생해요.

4) 누구의 말씀을 잘 들어야 합니까?

   부 모 님 의 말씀

5) 어떻게 부모님을 기쁘게 해드릴 수 있습니까?

   훌 륭 하 게 자라서

2. Change the sentences to the form shown below.

Ex. 나는 약을 먹는다.　→　나는 약을 먹어야 한다.

1) 나는 숙제를 한다.　→　나는 숙제를 해야 한다.

2) 아빠는 일하신다.　→　아빠는 일하셔야 한다.

3. Learn the Mother's Day song, "어머님 은혜."

높고 높은 하늘이라 말들 하지만 / 나는 높은 게 또 하나 있지
낳으시고 기르시는 어머님 은혜 / 푸른 하늘 그보다도 높은 것 같애.

211

수고
하셨습니다!

NOTE

NOTE

NOTE

NOTE